THE EPISTLE TO
THE HEBREWS

A Study Manual

by
GLEASON L. ARCHER, JR.

BAKER BOOK HOUSE
Grand Rapids 6, Michigan
1957

Dedicated to
Harold John Ockenga
Pastor of Park Street Church
Boston, Massachusetts
Who First Awakened in Me a Love
for the Systematic Study
of God's Word.

TABLE OF CONTENTS

THE PURPOSE OF THIS MANUAL

The purpose of this *Study Manual for the Epistle to the Hebrews* is quite specific. It is not intended to be a commentary in the usual sense of the word, since it does not discuss the conflicting views of the outstanding interpreters of this book, nor does it employ a Greek font in discussing the details of exegesis as a commentary properly should. Rather it is intended to serve the needs of a pastor or Bible teacher or even a college instructor in English Bible who desires a handy guide to the systematic exposition of this pivotal New Testament book in a form well adapted to the average student or parishioner. The main stress is laid upon a careful and elaborate outline, showing the logical progression of the thought of the Epistle from the standpoint of the central theme: the superiority of Christ to the angels, prophets and priests of the Old Covenant, and all that that entails in the way of superior resources for victorious living available to the New Testament Christian. The development of the Apostle's argument is carefully explained, as each proposition leads logically to the next. It is the conviction of the author of this Manual that the most significant work even in the line of expository messages can be accomplished only upon the basis of such a systematic development as this. Having grasped the total teaching of the book in relationship to its constituent parts, the preacher or teacher may select what chapters or paragraphs in *Hebrews* he feels would be most helpful to his hearers in the light of the number of meetings he has at his disposal for this series.

This outline study has been based upon a meticulous study of the Epistle in the original Greek, and of all the relevant Old Testament passages in the original Hebrew. The following commentaries have been consulted in the preparation of this Manual, and to them the reader is referred for more detailed information:

Marcus Dods: "The Epistle to the Hebrews" in *Expositor's Greek Testament,* vol. iv, (Hodder & Stoughton) 1917.

B. F. Westcott: "The Epistle to the Hebrews" (reprint) (Eerdmans) Grand Rapids, 1950.

A. B. Davidson: "The Epistle to the Hebrews" (reprint) (Zondervan) Grand Rapids, 1950.

Dr. Moll in J. P. Lange's "Commentary on the Holy Scriptures" (reprint) (Zondervan) Grand Rapids, n. d.

1

INTRODUCTION

Two important questions are dealt with in the Epistle to the Hebrews: the divine-human nature of Jesus Christ as our Mediator and High Priest, and the relationship between the Old Covenant and the New. To monotheistic Jews who naturally inclined towards unitarianism, the Apostle had to demonstrate from the Old Testament Scriptures themselves that Jesus Christ as the Son of God was no created being, not even the first being ever to be created by God (a view which later found expression in the great Arian heresy of the Fourth Century). On the contrary, He was the uncreated God Himself, the Second Person of the Trinity (although of course these theological terms were not employed until the time of Athanasius). And yet at the same time, as our Mediator, Jesus Christ was a true human being who partook of flesh and blood (2:14), that He might be qualified as a representative of the fallen race of mankind at the place of judgment on Golgotha. He presented Himself, then, as our High Priest and atoning sacrifice in the form of the God-Man, and not as an angelic being who took on human guise.

But also this Epistle deals with the question of the relationship of the Old Testament Scripture to the New Testament revelation. Was the Mosaic system of sacrifice and ritual still binding upon New Testament believers? The answer was No. Jesus Christ Himself has fulfilled all of the ceremonial Law, and thereby rendered obsolete all of the types and foreshadowing ordinances of the Old Covenant which pointed forward to Him as the great Antitype. Except as it illustrated and explained the nature of the transaction performed on Calvary, the ceremonial Law of the Old Testament became as obsolete as a bank check which has been cashed and canceled. All of the promises and the gracious deeds of deliverance and forgiveness wrought by God in behalf of His ancient people were conditioned upon the payment of the uniquely valid atonement price of the blood of Jesus Christ. Now that the payment has been made, shows the Apostle, we have entered upon a new order and enjoy a new standing before God as those for whom the ransom has already been paid.

And yet the finished work of atonement does not involve the obsolescence of the Old Testament as relevant and binding Scripture for the New Testament believer. On the contrary, the entire sacred collection of thirty-nine books glows with new

3

glory as a testimony to the person and work of the Mediator. It constitutes a collective document attesting the love of the Father for His Son and the marvelous provision He has made for the needs of His redeemed people through the ministry of His beloved Son. The Old Testament turns out to be a book all about the Son of God, and as such is a far more meaningful and blessed Scripture to the Christian than it could ever be to the unbelieving Jew.

The Church must ever revert to this sublime Epistle in order to bring the two Testaments into focus with each other. More than any other single book, *Hebrews* serves to demonstrate the underlying unity of the sixty-six books of the Bible as proceeding ultimately from the one and same divine author, the blessed Holy Spirit. The Church needs both Testaments if she is to be properly nourished on a well-rounded spiritual diet. The individual Christian needs to ponder *Hebrews* with reverent attention if he is to understand aright how all of Scripture focuses upon the person of his Savior, who has for him fulfilled the requirements of the Law, and has bestowed upon him by faith the Holy Spirit, who will enable him to follow in the train of Abraham, Moses and David, who though personally impotent became mighty instruments in the hand of an all-conquering God.

AUTHOR. Although the Authorized Version ascribes the authorship of *Hebrews* to the Apostle Paul, it is by no means certain that this tradition is correct. The Epistle does not begin with the identification of the writer and the apostolic salutation, as the thirteen other Pauline epistles do. The author speaks of himself (2:3) as belonging with his readers to the number of those who have received the Gospel at second hand from those who personally knew the Lord Jesus, and who have certified its divine authority by the testimony of miracles. This would have been extraordinary language for one like Paul, who had seen the Lord personally on several occasions, and had been personally instructed by Him by direct revelation (Gal. 1:12). Nor would Paul have by implication thus denied his apostolic authority, especially in writing to Hebrew Christians, who were of all people the most inclined to contest it. Moreover there are such differences of style and logical approach as to indicate very strongly a different author; Paul never employs the cultivated, literary diction and rhetorical polish which sets *Hebrews* in marked contrast to all of the other N. T. books.

The early church was quite divided in its opinion as to the true author of this epistle, even though the earliest post-canonical author, Clement of Rome, borrows from its language and imitates its expressions in such a way as to indicate that he knew the letter well and respected it as Scripture. Yet he does not quote from it by name or indicate the author, and the Western Church in general seems to have discounted claims to Pauline authorship. A North African tradition, represented by Tertullian, alleged that Barnabas was the true author (a theory also beset with difficulties, though none of them insuperable). In Alexandria and the East the tendency was to regard the Epistle as written by Paul himself, either directly in Greek or else in Hebrew Aramaic, from which it had been translated into Greek by none other than Luke (so Clement of Alexandria, about 200 A.D.). In trying to explain why Paul had not named himself as the apostolic author, Pantaenus of Alexandria (ca. 180 A.D.) suggested that Paul had suppressed his name on grounds of modesty, realizing that Christ Himself was the Apostle to the Jews, whereas he himself had received appointment only as apostle to the Gentiles. But even in the East, Origen of Alexandria (later of Caesarea, a martyr in the Decian persecution of 251) felt that the divergencies from the style which was characteristic of Paul's Greek made it impossible to regard him as the direct author; yet its general agreement with the teaching and thought of Paul made it likely to be a production of one of Paul's disciples. "But who wrote the Epistle God only knows certainly," he said. "The account that has reached us is twofold: some say that Clement, who became bishop of the Romans, wrote the Epistle, others that Luke wrote it, who wrote the Gospel and the Acts." These remarks are recorded for us by Eusebius, a disciple of Origen's, who however seemed to waver in his own opinion between Pauline authorship and classing it with the *antilegomena,* or books whose authority was questioned. Jerome (400 A.D.) was even more dubious about its origin, although Augustine was quite content to follow the Eastern tradition and class it as Pauline. In more recent times, Luther suggested that it was the work of Apollos (a view which has much to commend it, and accords well with what little we know of Apollos' background and approach), and others like Franz Delitzsch have advocated the ancient suggestion that Luke was the author. The mention of Timothy in 13:23 proves the writer to have been of the Pauline circle of acquaintance. Most present-day scholars, however, agree with Origen in the conclusion, "God only knows." At the same time it should be stressed that none of the ancient authorities above cited entertained any doubt as to the *canonicity* (i. e. the divine inspiration) of the Epistle. In any event the primary author of *Hebrews* is God Himself, no matter which human instrument He used in framing this Spirit-breathed and noble testimony to the Christian faith.

THE ADDRESSEES. This Epistle is addressed to Hebrew Christians belonging to some particular community or province of the Roman Empire, rather than to Jewish converts in general. This much is clear from the references made here and there (e. g. 6:10; 10:32-34; 12:4) to the present spiritual condition and past experiences and achievements of the addressees. But in what particular community did they dwell? It is a widely held opinion that they lived in Jerusalem itself, inasmuch as so much stress is laid upon sacrifice and ritual observance and high priestly intercession. Moreover, atmosphere and situation presupposed by the letter indicates an exclusively Jewish community, such as would not be found outside of the Jewish homeland itself.

There are, however, some very grave objections to this view, judging from various internal evidences in the Epistle itself. First, they are addressed in 2:3 as those who have received the Gospel at second hand; yet in Jerusalem itself even by 65 A.D. (the probable date of this letter) there must have been hundreds of church members who had heard the Gospel directly from the lips of Jesus Himself. They had received His message at first hand, if any church then existing could be said to have done so. Secondly, they are depicted as a spiritually backward church, still occupied with the first essentials of the Christian faith and not yet matured to an understanding of the deeper things of the Lord (5:12; 6:1-2). This would be very strange language to use of the mother church of all Christendom. Thirdly, they have endured much persecution of a moderate sort, such as public ridicule and reproach and loss of property (10:32-34), but they had not yet suffered actual martyrdom (12:4 "Ye have not resisted unto blood"). What a strange statement to address to the church which had produced Stephen, the very first martyr of them all, to say nothing of James the son of Zebedee! The references to tabernacle and sacrifice and high priest would have been relevant and appropriate whatever segment of Jewry was being addressed, for all Jews everywhere looked to the Mosaic ritual ordinances as their claim to special covenant relationship

6

with God, regardless of how infrequently they were able to attend the temple worship in person. Compare the relationship of Moslems to Mecca, whatever may be their home and country.

If then Jerusalem must be ruled out as the home of the readers of this Epistle, where else are they likely to have lived? The references in 13:24 to "they of Italy" is highly significant. Literally it says, "Those who are *from* Italy salute you," the preposition *apo* ("away from") suggesting that those who send salutations come from Italy originally and are sending their greetings back to the readers who dwell in Italy, rather than that they themselves now reside in Italy and send their salutations from Italy to the readers dwelling in some other land. For the latter idea Greek would be more apt to use the preposition *ek* ("out of, from"). If then the readers are being greeted in Italy by old friends who have migrated from Italy, it seems most likely that they constitute the large and influential Jewish segment of the Church at Rome. That they had returned in sufficient numbers to the imperial capital after the persecution under Claudius (Acts 18:2) to warrant such separate attention is attested by the large amount of attention given to them by Paul in his *Epistle to the Romans*. After his later arrival to Rome as a prisoner, Paul also had extensive dealings with the Jews themselves, as well as with Jewish Christians (many of whom had under Claudius doubtless suffered "the spoiling of their goods" Heb. 10:30). Since Timothy was with Paul during part, at least, of his imprisonment at Rome (cf. Phil. 1:1; Col. 1:1), the interest of the readers in Timothy's welfare can be readily understood. And lastly, the first extra-Biblical reference or allusion to *Hebrews* is found in the letter of Clement of Rome to the Corinthians, a fact easily explained if *Hebrews* reposed in the correspondence files of the Roman church.

TIME. The date of the Epistle may be narrowed down to the interval between the procuratorship of Gessius Florus in 64 A.D. and the outbreak of the First Revolt in 67 A.D. One generation of Christians had for the most part passed away, including all of the original leaders (13:7). There had been time enough since the first arrival of the Gospel message for the church in Rome to have passed beyond its earliest period of fervency and heroic zeal (5:11 ff.; 10:32). Yet the Levitical service was still being maintained at Jerusalem, as is evident from many passing references (8:4; 9:6,9; 10:1 ff.; 13:10 ff.). On the other hand, there is no reference whatever to the outbreak of the Jewish

7

War, a development of utmost significance, calling for pointed mention in the Eighth Chapter, where the transition from the Old Covenant to the New is under discussion. These factors seem to indicate a date of composition around 65 or 66 A.D. It seems clear that the Lord sent this revelation in order to prepare the Christian Church, and more specifically the Jewish members of it, for the epoch-making events connected with the Jewish Revolt and the final destruction of the Temple by the armies of Titus in the year 70 A.D. The Lord had withdrawn His protection from the Jewish sanctuary because it had been rendered obsolete by the high priestly work of Jesus Christ, who had expressly foretold its utter destruction in Matt. 24:2 (and the parallel passages).

OUTLINE OF THE EPISTLE TO THE HEBREWS

Subject:

The Superiority of Christ and the New Covenant

I. THE SUPERIORITY OF THE MEDIATOR (i-vii)

A. Christ's Superiority to the Prophets (i:1-3)
1. How special revelation came under Old Covenant (:1)
2. After this preparation God has spoken with finality through Christ (:2a)
3. Universal dominion bestowed upon the Son, His redeeming work accomplished (:2b)
4. Superiority of Christ as God incarnate (:3a-b)
5. His superiority as Messianic deliverer from sin (:3c)
6. His superiority in resurrection triumph over penalty of sin — death (:3d)

B. Christ's Superiority to Angels (i:4-ii:14)
1. Greater dignity bestowed on Him than on created beings (:4)
2. Proved by O.T. witness to superiority of Messiah to angels (:5-13)
   a. Ps. 2:7   b. II Sa. 7:14   c. Dt. 32:43   d. Ps. 104:4
   e. Ps. 45:7-8   f. Ps. 102:26-28   g. Ps. 110:1
3. In contrast to His Lordship, angels are mere servants for God and the elect (:14)
4. Christ's Gospel is therefore even more binding than Law mediated through angels (2:1-4)
5. Christ superior because the Kingdom has been committed to Him as God-Man (2:5-9)
6. The reason for and meaning of His humiliation and death as a human being (2:10)
7. This humiliation made Him a true member of the human race (2:11-13)
8. His humanity therefore made His Atonement effectual (2:14)
9. His victory through death set free men enslaved by fear of death (2:15)
10. His humanity made possible an effectual sacrifice and priesthood (:16-18)

C. Superiority of the Mediator to Moses (iii:1-6)
1. Christ was like Moses in faithfulness to God (:1-2)
2. But Moses was only a servant in a household created by Christ (:3-5)
3. Household of faith includes those of enduring faith (:6)

D. Superiority of Christ's Rest to the Rest of Moses and Joshua (Faith as Necessary Condition for Entrance) (3:7 - 4:13)
1. Faith necessary to enter Canaan, therefore also to enter the Kingdom (3:7-11)
2. To avoid tragic forfeiture of blessing, Christians need daily admonition (:12-13)
3. Only those who persevere in faith truly partake of Christ (:14-19)
4. Like the Israelites, Christians can enter the Rest by faith unshaken (4:1-2)
5. The Canaan-rest was a type, the reality of which yet lies before us (:3-8)
6. O.T. statements prove this antitypical Sabbath-rest awaits believers still (:9-10)
7. Christians must be zealous to enter it, avoiding the disobedience of the Exodus Israelites (:11)
   a. Sincere faith indispensable since God's Word and eye discerns the inmost soul of the professing believer (:12-13)
E. Superiority of the Son to Aaron as High Priest (iv:14-vii:28)
1. We may confidently approach God for grace, with Christ as High Priest (4:14-16)
2. High-priestly qualifications as typified in Mosaic ordinances (5:1-4)
3. How Christ fulfilled these qualifications, being appointed by God (:5-6)
4. How the Son fulfilled His high-priestly intercession for the Church (5:7-10)
5. Therefore Christians must lay hold with firm assurance upon what His propitiation has accomplished.
   a. Their backwardness reproved (:11-14)
   b. Need of advancing to maturer understanding (6:1-8)
      (1) We must advance from basic doctrines to maturer insights (:1-3)
      (2) Because it is useless to review first principles for those who have utterly rejected them and thus have no other provision of Grace to look to (:4-8)
   c. But the rest are ready for advanced teaching, and need not remain backward (:9-12)
   d. They are entitled to unshakable firmness under the covenant promise to Abraham and his seed (:13-20)
6. How the Melchizedek-priesthood surpasses that of Aaron (7:1-17)

a. The historical data and their typical significance (:1-3)
b. Superiority of Melchizedek-priesthood implied by Abraham's tithing (:4-10)
c. Would not have been ordained as a new order if Levitical priesthood was sufficient (:11-14)
d. Superior to Aaronic order because of immortality of the Antitype (:15-17)
7. The New Order resulting from the new Melchizedek-priesthood (7:18-22)
8. The complete efficacy of the Melchizedek-priesthood of Christ (7:23-28)

II. THE SUPERIORITY OF THE NEW COVENANT (viii:1-x:18)

A. The Evanescence of the Old Covenant (viii:1-13)
1. Christ's high-priestly work established the New Covenant (8:1-6)
2. The superior promises on which New Covenant is based (8:7-13)

B. The Spiritual Tabernacle and Sacrifice Supersede the Physical (ix)
1. Superiority of the N. T. heavenly Tabernacle to O. T. earthly Tabernacle (9:1-10)
   a. Contents of the earthly Tabernacle (the sacred furniture) (9:1-5)
   b. Difficulty of access to the Holiest Place (:6-8)
   c. The significance of this difficulty: mere physical symbol insufficient (:8-10)
2. Christ's service in the heavenly Tabernacle (:11-14)
3. The better Covenant and the better Sacrifice (:15-28)
   a. New Covenant based on death of Christ, not of beasts (:15)
   b. New Covenant-Testament validated by death of Victim-Testator (:16-17)
   c. Just as Old Covenant was validated by death — shed blood (:18-22)
   d. Once-and-for-all efficacy of Christ's single act of atonement (:23-28)

C. The Superiority and Finality of the New Covenant (x:1-18)
1. Finality of Christ's sacrifice cleanses conscience, brings men to God
   a. Old Covenant offered mere symbolic or provisional cleansing (:1-4)

11

2. Effectual and fulfilling nature of the sacrifice of Christ's body (:5-9)
3. Permanent effectiveness of His sacrifice means finality of His triumph (:10-13)
4. The Atonement works a complete transformation of the inner nature of believers (:14-18)

III. SUPERIOR RESOURCES FOR VICTORIOUS FAITH (x:19-xiii:25)

A. Encouragement to Hold Firm, Using New Access to God (x:19-39)
   1. Superior access to God, barriers removed through Messianic High Priest (:19-21)
   2. This access should be used by sanctified believers unhesitatingly (:22)
   3. Ground of confident affirmation: faithfulness of God who promised (:23)
   4. Result of holding to this confidence: encouragement of brother Christians in fruitful service (:24-25)
   5. Surpassing guilt of those who spurn this way of access; keep constant! (:26-39)
      a. Hopelessness of those who reject God's utmost for their redemption (:26-31)
      b. In view of past trials triumphantly endured, keep firm in faith (:32-35)
      c. In view of future heavenly reward, keep firm in faith! (:35b-39)

B. The Power of an Overcoming Faith Like the O. T. Heroes (xi)
   1. Essence of Faith: trust in the unseen God and His unfulfilled future promises (:1-3)
   2. Faith as exhibited by antediluvian Patriarchs (:4-7)
      a. Abel the Martyr: recognized man's natural obligations to God, even unto death (:4)
      b. Enoch the Immortalized: realized fellowship with God in godly living (:5-6)
      c. Noah the Righteous: obeyed God's specific orders and was saved through suffering (:7)
   3. Faith of the later Patriarchs: Faith in Relation to the People of God (:8-22)
      a. Abraham: the Faith of Patient Obedience (:8-19)
      b. Isaac, Jacob and Joseph: Faith of confidence in future fulfilment of God's Purpose (:20-22)

4. Faith of Moses: abandonment of worldly advantage for adversity in God's fellowship (23-31)
5. The Nation of Israel: Faith as found in its heroic Leaders and Prophets (:32-38)
   a. The open triumphs of faith (:32-35a)
   b. The victorious sufferings of faith (:35b-38)
   c. General characteristic: disregard of earthly values and the forward look to future fulfilment of God's promises.
C. The Surpassing Power of N. T. Faith, Based on Christ's Victory Already Won (xii)
   1. Victory through encouragement of Christ's example and the discipline of sonship (:1-11)
      a. Encouragement from these heroes who have proved the overcoming power of faith (:1)
      b. The supreme encouragement of Christ's example to cheerful endurance (:2-3)
      c. Chastisement proceeds from Paternal love and results in deepened spirituality (:4-11)
   2. Encouragement to harmony, holiness and care of the brethren (:12-17)
      a. Learning from the hardship, strive for peace with others and devotion towards God (:12-14)
      b. Care for fellow-Christians, that they avoid quarreling, inchastity or trifling away their inheritance (:15-17)
   3. N. T. sanctions for holy living even more binding than those of the O. T. (:18-29)
      a. Fearfulness of O. T. approach to indirect presence of God at Sinai (:18-21)
      b. Gloriousness of N. T. approach to direct presence of God in heavenly Zion (:22-24)
      c. A fortiori: even greater condemnation in disregarding Gospel than the Torah (:25)
      d. Hence we must reverently keep hold of Divine Grace, forsaking the temporal things of earth for immutable Kingdom of heaven (:26-29)
D. Surpassing Godliness Made Available by the Surpassing Power (xiii)
   1. Freedom from selfish niggardliness, self-centeredness, impurity and covetousness (:1-6)
   2. Respect for and imitation of the religious leaders of the church (:7)
   3. The unchanging Christ guarantees steadfastness in Christian doctrine (:8-9)

13

4. The privilege of separateness with Christ apart from the world (:10-14)
5. Heavenly citizenship involves duties of thanksgiving, benevolence and obedience to church leaders (:15-17)
6. Concluding requests and benedictions (:18-25)

I. SUPERIORITY OF THE MEDIATOR (Chaps. 1-7)

A. Christ's Superiority to the Prophets, the Mediators of the Old Covenant *(1:1-3)*.

1. **(1:1)** How special revelation came under the Old Covenant *(palai)*.

   a. By many portions *(polymerōs)*, i. e. part by part in progressive stages, first to Adam, then Noah, then Abraham, then Moses, etc.

   b. By many different methods *(polytropōs)*: by signs, by types, by prophetic events, by sermons and psalms — all of these being recorded for us in the Written Word (O. T.) by the writing prophets.

2. **(1:2a)** The new revelation: at the end of the preparatory ages. God has with finality spoken through His Son. (Christ as Prophet)

   a. Note that "at the end of these days" (AV: "in these last days") renders the common O. T. phrase *be'aherith hayyāmim* ("in-the-end-of-the-days"), which usually connotes the days of the Messiah (so acknowledged by the Rabbis, such as Kimchi).

   b. Christ's Gospel, therefore, is uniquely valid, the focal point toward which all previous revelation has tended; the key to a coherent and meaningful understanding of the O. T., with its preliminary revelations and foreshadowings.

   c. Note: the Greek here says "by *a* Son" *(en huiō)*, not "by *the* Son" or "by *His* Son" (although both of these statements would have been true), for the important truth to bring out here is that the absolute and final revelation came not by a man or an angel (as it had previously) but by One who was generically different, a *Son;* that is, the unique Son of God, who is Himself God (as the Apostle proceeds to make clear).

3. **(1:2b)** At this final time God has bestowed the domain of the universe upon His Messianic Son. Hence He is *superior* because of His universal Lordship. All God the Father has now belongs to the God-Man, who has spoken, redeemed and risen.

4. **(1:3a-b)** Superiority of Christ as Second Person of the Trinity.

a. Creator of the universe at the beginning; He made the *aiōnes* ("world-ages," "worlds"), or the aggregate of all things contained in time.

b. Visible manifestation or "brightness" *(apaugasma)* of the glory of the Godhead. Note: *apaugasma* means "effulgence" or "reflection," i. e. the rays of light emitted by the original luminary and forming a sort of light-body of their own. (So Athanasius pointed out that this term proves that Christ was eternally generated, and does not exist by an act of the Father's will, but rather exists essentially. As the sun cannot exist without radiating light, so the Godhead is essentially Father and Son.)

Glory equals *doxa,* "appearance" or "manifestation" — that which is displayed to the eye (but not necessarily the entire thing in itself, or the entire nature of God in His essence). This *doxa* corresponds to the O. T. *kābōd* ("glory," "honor," "splendor"), a term applied to the glory-cloud (pillar of cloud and fire) which accompanied the Israelites during the Exodus, and rested over the mercy-seat in the Tabernacle.

c. "Express image" or precise reproduction in every respect *(kharaktēr)* of the "person" or essential nature *(hypostasis* — underlying reality) of God. Literally, *kharaktēr* was applied to the wax impression made by a signet ring, for the wax fitted perfectly into the features of the mould impressed upon it. (Note: this use of *hypostasis* as "substance" or essential nature, differs from the later technical use of the word by the Greek authors after the Nicene Council, to mean "person" of the Trinity.)

d. Sustainer of all the created universe ("upholding all things") — which is only maintained in existence by the command of His will, and which is controlled by His providence and sovereign decree, and that too towards a praiseworthy outcome, a God-glorifying goal (involving the Incarnation and Atonement).

Note that "upholding" *(pherōn)* literally means "carrying," and therefore implies movement and progress towards a goal.

"By the *word* of His power": this is *rhēma* (rather than *logos*), expressing a particular act or command of divine Providence. *(Logos* is a more general term for speech or discourse or the giving oral expression to what is in the mind — hence a very fitting term for Christ in John 1:1, where *Word* sets forth the Son as the expression of what is in the mind of the Father.)

5. **(1:3c)** Superiority of Christ as Messianic Deliverer from sin. (Christ as priest)
   a. He did not merely *promise* forgiveness, as did the prophets of the O. T., but He actually effectuated forgiveness (lit.: "having performed for Himself purification," translated as, "when He had by Himself purged"). He purged away our sins, which required forgiveness and removal. Note here an implied contrast to the imperfect Levitical sacrifices — a theme taken up in Chap. 10.
   b. It was He who did the removing; man cannot remove his own sins by resolving to do better, or by espousing higher ideals, under the moral influence of the Atonement.

6. **(1:3d)** Christ's superiority as the Resurrected One, the Victor over death, the penalty for sin. (Christ as King)
   a. Now He sits as Lord of all, not simply as God the Son (as He was prior to the Incarnation) but as the Messianic God-Man, who not only has power over sin to punish it, but also power over sin to extinguish it and replace it by His own nature, in the heart of rebellious man (now conquered by His love).
   b. "On the right hand of the Majesty on high" suggests fulfilment of the promise of Ps. 110:1 "Jehovah said unto my Lord: Sit Thou on My right hand, until I make Thine enemies Thy footstool." The man who sat at the right hand of a king was the most powerful and authoritative subject in the kingdom. Because Christ sits at the right hand of God, "all authority in heaven and in earth" has been committed to Him (Mat. 28:18). In heaven He sits as King already, even though He has not yet occupied the throne of David, as He shall do in the Millennial Kingdom which is yet to come (Is. 9:7).
   c. Because He sits at God's right hand, He is supreme, and therefore no difficulty on earth is a problem to

17

Him. He has everything well in hand and can answer any prayer of God's children.

B. Christ's Superiority to Angels *(1:4-2:14)*.

1. **(1:4)** Because He has received a greater dignity and authority than that bestowed upon any created beings, the authority bestowed upon Him as the Second Adam, who has by fulfilling the Law obtained the dominion promised to the first Adam had he kept the Law.

But of course a far greater authority than that, since as God-Man He rules over the entire created universe, not just this planet.

Note: "Hath obtained by inheritance" or "has inherited" *(keklēronomēke)* points to the Covenant-term, "inheritance" *(klēronomia)*, first mentioned in God's promises to Abraham of Canaanland, but then enlarged to the entire world in Ps. 2:8 ("I will give Thee the heathen for Thine inheritance — *nahalah)*.

a. Specifically, He has inherited a name, the Name by which alone sinners may be saved (Acts 4:12) and at which every knee shall bow (Phil. 2:10). Angels cannot save sinners, nor do they bear supreme authority, only delegated authority. Only the name of Jesus casts out evil spirits. It is the most potent, miracle-working name in the universe. From its O. T. background, the word "name" (Gr. *onoma,* Heb. *shēm)* includes the notions of (1) glory, reputation among men (2) a man's character as recognized and made known to others by his conduct and demeanor (as God made known His Name by His acts of redemption during the Exodus, and by His judgments upon Egypt and the heathen). (G. Oehler: "The name of God denotes all the operations of God through which He attests His personal presence in that relation into which He has entered with man; i. e. the whole of the divine self-manifestation, or that side of the divine nature which is turned towards men.") (3) a man's authority as ruler or magistrate (e. g. to cast out demons in the *name* of Jesus of Nazareth).

2. **(1:5)** This is the united testimony of the O. T., which clearly distinguishes Messiah as superior to angels.

a. Proved by Ps. 2:7: "My Son art Thou; I Myself this day ("this day" refers to the time of the Incarnation, which appears to the inspired Psalmist as taking place before his mind's eye) have begotten Thee." This is specifically addressed to the Messiah.

   (1) Angels are, to be sure, called "sons of God" in Ps. 29:1; 89:7; Job 1:6; but always as a group or class, never as individuals. Therefore Christ was in a peculiar sense *the* Son of God, in a special way begotten by God.

b. **(1:5b)** Proved by II Sam. 7:14: "I Myself will be to him for a Father, and he himself shall be to Me for a son." This was an assurance to David concerning his descendant. Hence the ultimate object of this promised blessing was not Solomon as such, but only as a type and ancestor of the Messianic Prince of Peace (cf. Ps. 72:8; Zec. 9:10).

c. **(1:6)** Proved by Ps. 97:7b: "Prostrate yourselves to Him, all ye gods" (where "gods" — *'elōhim* — refers to those in God's family, even as "Israel" is applied to those in Israel's — Jacob's — family and descendants; cf. what Jesus said in John 10:34-35). Note that the Greek O. T., the Septuagint (abbreviated as "LXX") here translated "gods" by "angels."

   (1) This shows that the angels are inferior to the Son, and obliged to adore Him as God.

   (2) This Psalm prophetically introduces the Messianic Son as heir — the "firstborn," the eldest and foremost son — as conqueror at His Second Advent (if we are to connect the adverb "again" with "He bringeth . . . into," as the Greek here permits). Note that this application of Ps. 97 assumes that it describes the Second Person of the Trinity, as the "fire" and the "lightnings" and the "presence" of Jehovah. This conspicuous manifestation of God, this display of His "glory" (Ps. 97:6) corresponds to what has just been said of Christ as the "brightness" (Heb. 1:3) of God's image.

d. **(1:7)** Proved by Ps. 104:4: "Making His messengers/angels *(mal'ākhim)* winds/spirits *(rūhōth)*, His servants a flaming fire." Here it is again made clear that angels are to serve as subordinates and worshippers, rather than being worshipped and adored as sovereign, the way the Messiah is.

e. **(1:8-9)** Proved by Ps. 45:7-8:

(1) **(:7a)** "Thy throne, O God, is forever and ever." This means that the Son is the heavenly King whose rule is eternal. Note that Ps. 45 begins: "My heart is inditing a good matter: I speak . . . of the King . . . Thou art fairer than the children of men." Obviously it is a human king who is being spoken of, yet he is in Verse Seven addressed as God. This can apply only to the God-Man, enthroned as Sovereign in His heavenly glory.

(2) **(:7b)** "A scepter of justice is the scepter of Thy kingdom" — showing that the Messianic King is holy and righteous in the way He rules over heaven and earth.

(3) **(:8a)** "Thou lovest righteousness and hatest wickedness." This adherence to the holy standard of divine righteousness *(sedeq)* is based not upon enlightened self-interest, but upon a sincere love of the Law for its own sake, as the expression of God's perfect will; and also upon a sincere hatred for sin. Both of these attitudes are beyond the capacity of fallen man.

(4) **(:8b)** "God has anointed Thee with the oil of rejoicing . . ." Therefore the Son, as the God-Man, has been anointed as victor on a day of jubilant triumph, in preference to or above all His "fellows" (Heb. *hebārim*: "associates" or "companions"; rendered here by the Greek *metokhoi*: "sharers" or "those who have a part in something with someone else"). This shows that God makes a great distinction in position and glory as between the Messiah and the angels.

f. Proved by Ps. 102:26-28 (Heb. 1:10-12)

(1) **(:25)** "The earth hast Thou founded, and the workmanship of Thy hands are the heavens." Here the Messiah is addressed as the Creator. Ps. 102:16 shows that these remarks do pertain to Christ: "When Jehovah shall build up Zion, He shall appear in His glory." This suggests that God appears and comes in the person of the Son, and therefore it is the Son who is addressed as Creator in Verse 26. (Creation is the prerogative of God alone.)

20

(2) **(:26)** "These shall pass away, but Thou shalt remain." That is, the heavens themselves, being part of creation, shall pass away, but this Messiah shall eternally endure even thereafter.

(3) **(:27)** "But Thou art the same, and Thy years shall not fail (be used up)." The unchangeableness of Christ in His character is emphasized here, as well as His endless eternity (cf. Heb. 13:8).

g. **(1:13)** Proved by Ps. 110:1 (which was already alluded to in 1:3) : "Sit Thou at My right hand, until I make Thine enemies Thy footstool." This verse shows that the Messiah, in contrast to the angels, is seated as Supreme Ruler, the God-Man to whom God has delegated the authority to rule over all, with a guarantee of ultimate triumph over all who oppose Him. (Wonderful assurance, blessed comfort to beleaguered Christians who are being persecuted and even martyred because they give their first loyalty to Christ!)

3. **(1:14)** In contrast to all of these characteristics of Creatorship and Lordship attributed by the O. T. to the Messiah, the angels are described as mere subordinates, servants of God, used by God for the blessing of the chosen and redeemed descendants of Adam. Their principal occupation is to serve man. [Note that they are "ministering" spirits, *leitourgika pneumata*, but not "servants" in the usual sense of slaves *(douloi)*. As *leitourgoi* ("ministers") the angels are like freemen who have voluntarily entered into the employ of another. But Christ Himself in His humiliation as our Redeemer, presented Himself as a "servant" in the sense of "bondslave" *(doulos)*, according to the teaching of Phil 2:7.]

4. **(2:1-4)** Therefore the Gospel — Christ's message — is of even greater sanctity and binding force than the O. T. Law itself, which was mediated to Moses by mere angels.

a. **(2:2)** The O. T. Law demanded and received the utmost of reverent attention from God's people, who studied it day and night (Jos. 1:8; Ps. 1:2) and accounted it more precious than gold (Ps. 19:10). Moreover this O. T. Law was supernaturally vindicated by God, who meted out exemplary punishment to Nadab and Abihu (Lev. 10:1-7), to Korah, Dathan and Abiram (Num. 16), to Achan (Jos. 7), and also, by predicted historical judgments, the Kingdoms of Judah

21

and Israel. Thus the Law when violated brought upon the violators exactly the penalties which it threatened.

b. **(2:3b-4)** But the N. T. Gospel — the fulfilling of the Law — is of an even greater sanctity, validity and inviolability than was the O. T. Law.

    (1) Because it was proclaimed by the Messiah, the Lord Himself.

    (2) Next, because it was proclaimed by the Apostles whom He had taught and sent; and also because when it was spoken by them, it was accompanied by a power to convict and convert sinners.

    (3) Lastly, because it was authenticated by the power of the Holy Spirit, as He performed: (a) testimony-miracles *(sēmeia — "signs")* such as the stilling of the storm; (b) wonder-miracles *(terata — "wonders")* such as the feeding of the 5000; (c) various types of power-miracles *(dynameis — "miracles")* such as the casting out of demons; (d) spiritual gifts and capacities distributed *(merismoi — distributions, "gifts")* to born-again Christians, such as prophecy, powers of healing, etc. (I Cor. 12:10 ff.)

c. **(2:1)** Warning: therefore take heed, lest you be carried away or drift past *(pararreō)* the sure anchorage which is within reach. (This is a warning all the more needful because the Gospel involves a removal of the yoke of the Law, and therefore leaves room for the immature or insincere to become fatally careless and fail to take God seriously.)

5. **(2:5-9)** Christ is superior to the angels because the government of the future Millennial Kingdom has been committed to Him, as the Messianic God-Man, the Second Adam. (Even though man is naturally inferior to angels, nevertheless this Man is superior, because victor over death and Lord of the Kingdom to come.)

a. **(2:5-7)** Proved by Ps. 8:5-7, which speaks of the privileged status of man over the rest of creation on earth, yet in terms hyperbolic for Adam's race. But this turns out to have a literal application to the Second Adam, for truly to Him all the universe has been subjected by God the Father. Not to the angels, even though they do have a share in making God's rule

22

effectual (e. g. Michael is especially assigned to defend Israel according to Dan. 9 and 12).

b. **(2:8)** But not all things have as yet been literally subjected to Christ (i. e. the disobedient world of men and demons). This part of the prophecy of Ps. 8 has yet to be consummated in connection with the Millennial Kingdom.

c. **(2:9a)** Yet its fulfilment is guaranteed by the portion of the prophecy already fulfilled: already Christ has been resurrected from that death which was the utmost ill His foes could inflict upon Him (and which of course lowered Him below the level of the immortal angels), and has been exalted to supreme glory in heaven.

d. **(2:9b)** Strangely enough, this exaltation of the God-Man was only brought to pass by His prior humiliation: the Incarnation and the Cross. (Now the apostle shows why the humiliation of Christ was warranted.)

    (1) His death was vicarious, i. e. on behalf of every man "who believeth."

    (2) His achieving of glory and honor means that all those in Him by faith likewise partook of them.

6. **(2:10)** The reason for and significance of Christ's humanity and death as a human being.

a. God performed this redemption of the elect by fully preparing and qualifying the Messiah through His sufferings as a human being.

    (1) This humiliation was not contrary to God's nature or glory (although this was the great stumbling-block to the Jews), but rather it was fully expressive of God's true nature (as loving and compassionate), even though He is the Transcendent Lord and Creator of all things, and the reason for the existence of all things that are.

    (2) This permitting of Christ's humiliation was motivated by God's purpose to redeem men and make them by grace His sons, thus causing them to share in the glory of His Kingdom.

    (3) Until the redemptive sufferings were endured, Christ was not yet perfectly qualified to function as founder (or "captain" — *arkhēgos*, literally "the beginning-leader") of their salvation. (Note that

this same *arkhēgos* occurs in 12:2 as the originator or founder of the Christian's faith; there it is translated "author.")

    (i)   Not until the Second Federal Head of mankind, the Representative of believing sinners, had actually fulfilled the Law by obeying where Adam, the first Federal Head, had disobeyed, was it possible for God justly to acquit the race of the redeemed, while at the same time upholding and safeguarding the validity of His holy Law against the assaults of sin and rebellion.

    (ii)   By His perfect fulfilling of the Law, the Redeemer only made Himself personally approved as holy; to be completely qualified as the victorious liberator of the chosen people, He had to offer up His own life in their place. This He could do only by the suffering of death. Hence these sufferings were necessary for the full qualifying of the God-Man as our victor and liberator.

7. **(2:11-13)** This humanity of Christ was genuine, making Him a true member of the human race, rather than God in human disguise (even though He continued to be the Eternal God, the Second Person of the Trinity).

  a. **(:11a)** "For both He who sanctifies (us sinners) — i. e. Jesus Christ — and those who are sanctified — i. e. we Christians — are all of (*ek*, "out of") One (Father)." The Messiah was in His human nature begotten of God into the same human race as we have been.

  b. **(:11b)** Even though the Messiah is in His divine nature God the Son, and not simply a son of God by adoption as believers are, yet as Man Christ does not hesitate to class Himself as our brother.

    (1) **(:12)** This is proved by Ps. 22:23, where Christ says: "I shall proclaim Thy name to My brethren." In this Messianic Psalm, the words of which can apply only to Him in their fullest sense, He takes His stand with redeemed believers from Adam's race, joining with them in adoration and praise of the Father. (Note the doctrine of inspiration here assumed: that the pre-incarnate Son inspired these words in David as he wrote, so that they had only

24

partial application to David by way of poetic hyperbole, but full application only to the One whom David typified, "great David's greater Son." Thus the pre-incarnate Christ indicated in advance what He as incarnate God and Son of man would feel and say upon the Cross.)

(2) **(:13a)** Proved also by Is. 8:17: "And I shall be reposing my confidence in Him" (Heb. "And I shall wait-expectantly for Him"). These words were spoken by Isaiah not simply in his own capacity but in his capacity as a type of the Messiah. Christ here assumes the same position of faith and trust in God which human believers must occupy. (The Gospel record relates many an utterance of Jesus testifying to His attitude of dependence upon the Father, even in the performance of miracles. He did not perform them by His own divine power as God the Son, but only by faith in response to prayer. "The works that I do shall ye do also" (John 14:12).

(3) **(:13b)** Proved by Is. 8:18: "Behold I and the children which Thou (O Father) hast given Me are for signs and wonders in Israel." Here again we see that Isaiah was speaking as a type of the Messiah, and the words he spoke here apply to Him whom He typified. Note that the name Isaiah (*Yesha'yāhū*) means "The salvation of Jehovah," and thus has the same component words in it as "Jesus," which is the Greek form of "Joshua" (the longer form of which is *Yeho-shua'* — "Jehovah is salvation." Only Christ could make possible such a prophet as Isaiah; as the Living Word it was He who inspired him and directed him what to say and do, giving him the clearest revelation of the Atonement and the Cross to be found anywhere in the O. T. — i. e. in his 53rd chapter. As for Isaiah's children, Shear-jashub means "A Remnant shall Return," which indicates that Christ's covenant children shall be composed of only the repentant few of professing believers who are truly repentant, born-again believers; the younger son, Maher-shalal-hash-baz, had a name meaning "Hurry to the Plunder, Haste to the

Spoil," signifying the victorious, fruit-bearing, soul-winning life of true believers in Christ.

8. **(2:14)** This true humanity of Christ made His Atonement effectual.

   a. **(:14a)** Since the Messiah, to be a proper representative of man at the Cross of judgment, had to partake of a genuine human nature like that of those whom He was representing, and for whom He was being substituted as Sin-bearer, it was necessary for Him to become a real, flesh-and-blood human being (rather than assuming a mere human disguise, as the heretical Docetists taught, or having a nature only partially human, as the Apollinarians taught).

   b. **(:14b)** Christ likewise partook of flesh and blood, that He might "destroy" (*katargeō* — "render inoperative," "put to naught") the power of Satan, the Prince of Death. As God, of course, Christ could not die, and therefore could not atone; as Man He could suffer death, and thus present the Law-satisfying sacrifice for those of whom He was a representative. This apparent defeat or discreditation of the Messiah became the very means by which Satan was rendered impotent, though he exercises the rule (*kratos* "power") over death. The death of the sinless Substitute meant full payment for all those who become united with Christ by faith, and who therefore have paid the death penalty in Him. Satan has no authority to demand death a second time from the same person; therefore he has no dominion over those who have already died (by representation) in Christ.

9. **(2:15)** This victory by death had the effect of setting free (*apallassō*) men who were enslaved to the fear of death (since sin had to be accounted for and death loomed up as the punishment for it). Note that as long as man has to worry about escaping hell, he will be self-seeking in all his motivation, even in his religion. Only when man, having been redeemed, no longer needs to be concerned about himself, is he set free for a life of self-disinterested benevolence.

10. **(:16-18)** This humanity of Christ qualified Him as a Savior only by way of an effectual atoning sacrifice and an effectual priesthood. (This hints at a theme to be developed later in the Epistle.)

a. **(:16)** His saving ministry was only to mankind, not to angels, for He came to reach out a helping hand to (or to succor — *epilambanomai*) the children of Abraham (AV's "took on . . . the nature of" seems to be inaccurate for *eptilambanomai*).

b. Therefore He became a true human being and an Israelite, subject to the limitations of finiteness and physical weakness, like mankind in general. Thus He became eligible to be chosen from among them to serve as their representative and priest.

c. **(2:17)** Being subject to their limitations and thus capable of bearing the brunt of temptation such as assail other men, the Messiah was in a position to be faithful (because united in interest with His redeemed) and also merciful (because understanding from within the human family what their weaknesses and motives are) and yet at the same time be perfectly true to God's interests and concerns. Therefore He was fully qualified as a mediator, and His propitiation (the satisfaction He offered for the broken Law) was valid and effectual.

d. **(2:18)** Having overcome temptation as man's representative and Federal Head, Christ is able to supply imputed righteousness so as to cancel out the debt of sin, and provide an indwelling holiness to break the power of sin within the human heart.

C. The Superiority of the Mediator to Moses *(3:1-6)*

1. **(3:1-2)** Christ resembled Moses in faithfulness and in utter devotion to God. [Note the following: The readers of this Epistle are addressed (i) as *brethren*, because members of the same holy family as the Apostles, and born again by the same Holy Spirit; (ii) as "holy" *(hagioi)* because clothed with Christ's righteousness, set apart for God's use, and indwelt by His Holy Spirit; (iii) as "partakers of the heavenly calling," because God has called them out of the world to be His own children, whose proper home is therefore in heaven, His dwelling-place; thus the call came down from heaven and leads those who are effectually called to heaven as their abode. This suggests a theme to be discussed later, the "rest" that God has for the saints.]

a. They are to "consider" *(katanoeō* — "observe so as to

see the significance of") this Lord Christ as: (i) "the Apostle of our profession" — cf. Jn. 20:21: "As the Father hath sent *(apestalken)* Me, so send I *(apostellō)* you"; an *apostolos* is one who has been sent off on a mission by someone in authority, and so Jesus is the Father's Apostle, even as Christ sent His disciples off on His mission, making them thus His apostles. (ii) "High Priest of our confession" — i. e. Whom we acknowledge and confess before men to be our High Priest. The Aaronic high priest was the person who represented the whole nation before God, as he offered by blood-sacrifice an atonement for their sins, being the only one permitted to enter God's immediate presence before the Ark on the Day of Atonement. (This also introduces a theme to be more fully developed later on.)

    b. The point of resemblance between Christ and Moses is that they both were absolutely faithful to God, cherishing no interests or aims aside from those of Jehovah Himself.

2. **(3:3-5)** The point of contrast between them: Moses was only a servant *(therapōn* — "a hired domestic") within the household of faith, whereas Christ was the very Creator of the household, both by the original creation (John 1:3) and by the New Creation.

    a. Moses, on the one hand, was a faithful servant, serving within the household; not being himself the fulfilment of God's promises, he could only act as a witness to the promises of the future redemption of God's people.

    b. Christ, on the other hand, was appointed by the Father as His Son and Heir to whom all the Father's property descends by right of inheritance, so that He stands in exactly the same position of Lordship as His Father.

3. **(3:6)** The significance of the "house" *(oikos)*: the company of redeemed believers, i. e. those truly of the elect, who have received a permanent and unshakable faith in God. (This suggests a distinction between saving faith and a vain faith which is the next theme to be developed.)

D. The Superiority of Christ's Rest to the Rest of Moses and Joshua *(3:7-4:13)*

1. **(3:7-12)** Faith was a necessary qualification for entrance into Canaan, and therefore also into the Kingdom of God.

28

a. **(3:7-11)** The Scripture-passage which establishes this truth: Ps. 95:7-11: "Today, if you hearken to His voice, do not harden your hearts as in the Provocation (Heb. *Meribah* — "Place or Act of Controversy"), on the day of testing in the wilderness, when your fathers tested (Me) with a putting-to-the-proof *(dokimasia)* and beheld My deeds for forty years (thereafter); on account of which I was indignant at this generation and said, 'They are always erring in their heart, and they themselves have not come to know My ways; as I have taken oath in My anger, they shall surely not enter into My rest.'" (Here the Hebraic oath-formula is literally translated into Greek: "*If* they shall enter. . . ." The "if" is equivalent to a negative oath, just as we say: "If I ever let you touch that again, then my name is not John Smith"; only in Hebrew, the "then . . ." clause is omitted, and merely implied.) This passage brings out the following points: (i) true obedience goes beyond a mere hearing of instructions; (ii) it stands in contrast to the hardening of the heart in self-will; (iii) on the Day of Provocation they challenged God's sovereignty by rebelling against Him, i. e. at Kadesh Barnea (Num. 20) in connection with the running out of their water-supply, and that too after they had (in Num. 14) refused to enter Canaan because of the Report of the Ten Spies; (iv) such a heart-hardening brought on a general failure to recognize and understand God's ways, despite the utmost clarity of revelation to them through Moses on Mt. Sinai; (v) this wilful ignorance and disobedience compelled God to shut them out of His "rest," i. e. the goal of victory and blessedness in the Land of Promise.

b. **(3:12)** Therefore you Hebrew Christians must also beware of presuming upon your status under the Covenant, so as to suppose that you can be careless and fall short of real submission to God. A basic lack of faith might then arise, to prompt you to desert ("in departing" — Gr. *apostēnai*, from which we derive the word *apostasy*) from God's camp to join the forces of His foes.

2. **(3:13)** Therefore to avoid this tragic desertion and loss of blessing, Christians must admonish and encourage

(*parakaleō*) one another constantly, humbly seeking God's redeeming grace day by day.

a. **(:13b)** A daily admonition is all the more needful because sin does not always betray its true nature ("the *deceitfulness* of sin"), but comes disguised as something allowable or legitimate, and then, when yielded to, it lends itself to palliating extenuation and a consequent hypocrisy and heart-hardening against the known will of God.

3. **(3:14-19)** Apostasy is a present possibility and a very real danger, since of course only those who do not apostatize are true believers who really do partake of Christ. It is only true believers who retain their firm assurance in God to the end of their lives. (Implication: an assurance of faith may be lost through wilful neglect or disobedience.)

a. **(3:16)** (This standard of persevering faith and willingness to obey must not be relaxed, for:) the whole generation who came up out of Egypt, though they began well, later provoked God by their unbelief and disobedience. (Note: God did not at that time lower His standards to suit the level of the majority.) (Observe also: the only kind of god who would not have been provoked would have been a god who is relatively indifferent to sin and only mildly concerned to defend his moral law.)

b. **(3:17a)** The grace of God does not amount to pretending that sin is no longer sin; His wrath is upon sinning (i. e., self-deifying) professing Christians, as well as non-professing sinners.

c. **(3:17b-18)** The needless tragedy was that they who could have entered into the fulness of the Christian experience, i. e. the generation who heeded the report of the Ten Spies, were left behind in the desert as corpses, instead of marching in with Joshua.

d. **(3:19)** They refused to believe that God could bring them into the Promised Land in the face of powerful human opposition, and therefore would not go forward. They were rendered weak and incapable by their failure to trust in God's promises. (So also the Hebrew Christians stood in danger of shrinking from further conflict with their compatriots, and so of losing all they had apparently won.)

4. **(4:1-2)** Like the Israelites of Moses' day, Christians also are able to enter the promised rest only by steadfast faith.
   a. If God's promise is neglected, you too will come short (i. e. fall like corpses in the wilderness); for God's promise must not only be heard but also believed.

5. **(4:3-8)** The spiritual Promised Land lies yet before us, for the O. T. teaches that the Canaan-rest was prophetic of a larger fulfilment. As Christians enter into Christ's resurrection life and activity, they enter into the spiritual reality typified by that rest.
   a. **(4:3b-5)** Proved by Ps. 95:11, which implies that those Israelites not under wrath because of unbelief may enter into the spiritual "rest" of God. This is shown by comparison with Gen. 2:2, which states that God back at the time of creation rested from His physical creative work. Consequently the "rest" mentioned in Ps. 95 must have been meant spiritually, not physically or materially. (From this it follows that the Promised Land itself was a type of a heavenly commonwealth far transcending the earthly in importance.)
   b. **(4:6)** Ps. 95:11 proves not only that there yet remains a spiritual antitype of the Canaan-rest, but also that it may be entered into only by true believers.
   c. **(4:7)** Ps. 95:11 also proves that this spiritual rest is to be entered into now, in the Messianic era in which we now live.
   d. **(4:8)** The promise of rest made to the Exodus-generation could not have been completely fulfilled under Joshua in his conquest of Canaan, or else the much later Ps. 95 would not have spoken of this rest as a present ("today") and future possibility.

6. **(4:9-10)** The antitypical character of this rest promised to believers: these O. T. passages prove that there is a Sabbath-rest, analogous to the Creation-rest of God, and appointed for believers even today.
   a. The typical fulfilment: God rested from His work of creation on the Seventh Day, because He had reached an accomplished purpose. So also when believers enter Christ's Kingdom by faith, they too rest from their own works (and efforts to attain righteousness by works) and enter into the realm of attainment of accomplished purpose.

b. Most scholars regard this simply as a type of heaven itself, and it is doubtless true that heaven is implied. But this "rest" cannot simply refer to heaven, inasmuch as it is clearly implied by v. 11 that we shall escape falling by the same example of unbelief once we have entered into the Lord's "rest," and that this "rest" is a haven into which we should here and now in this life seek to enter. An encouragement to seek early death (the indispensable means of attaining heaven) would hardly be appropriate here.

7. **(4:11-13)** Since therefore this spiritual rest lies before us and can only be entered by true believers, let us be zealous to enter into it, thus avoiding the evil example of the Exodus-generation, who failed to enter in because of disobedience.

a. This great carefulness and zeal is all the more needful because we know how clearly the Lord Christ and the Bible (as the written Word of Christ) see into our innermost motives and can discern whether we truly believe and mean to obey God.

(Note: we are not to understand by "the word of God" here the Lord Jesus Himself to the exclusion of His spoken and written word, but rather the Lord and His word communicated through His messengers and applied by the Holy Spirit to the heart of the believer. Cf. John 12:48: "The word that I have spoken, the same shall judge him in the last day." After all, Christ Himself is not the "sword," but rather, it is the word which issues from His mouth with judicial power; cf. Rev. 1:16.)

b. The operation of Christ's penetrating Word:

  (i) This Word is "quick," or "living," i. e. efficacious and operative, even as it was when it first issued from the Lord's mouth. *Life* is characterized by activity, here taking the special form of internal examination which reaches to the very foundations of us. It is living because instinct with the life of its divine source.

  (ii) It is also "powerful" (*energēs* — effectively operative; from this we get the English word "energy"); that is, the *life* is translated into efficacious operation, really accomplishing the work it is intended to do (cf. Is. 55:11).

32

(iii) It is also "sharper" (*tomōteros* — "more cutting") than any literal sword, since it is able to penetrate what man-made swords never can: the human soul.

(iv) This sword of the Word cuts until it divides the soul and spirit of man even to their very joints and marrow, so to speak; that is to say, even to their most secret recesses, thus laying bare even their most hidden movements and basic structure. The comments of Franz Delitzsch at this point are most illuminating. He says in effect: The "soul" and "spirit" represent the invisible and supersensuous part of man, the "joints and marrow" the perceptible and sensuous. The Word of God penetrates to exhibit to man the monstrous breach between his soul and body. The "joints," which subserve bodily motion, and the "marrows" (*myeloi* is plural) which minister to bodily sensation, are exhibited as being wrought upon by ungodly forces so as to become the seat of death. This whole man, thus described, is laid bare before God and before himself as well, showing him in what degree he has not truly yielded to the work of Grace.

(v) This Word is able at all times to distinguish and pass judgment upon the "thoughts" (*enthymēseis* includes "emotions, notions, fancies") and "intents" (*ennoiai* or "self-conscious trains of thought") which proceed from the "heart" (*kardia*: that personal point of unity from which arise all the activities of mind, emotion and bodily faculties).

(vi) This Word is able to perform this judgment because of its perfect insight into every part of a man's soul, which finds itself utterly unable to conceal or put a favorable appearance upon anything unworthy in it. All of a man's inner thoughts and emotions and motives are uncovered and unclothed (*gymna*) and completely exposed to God's view, or "open" (*tetrakhēlismena*, literally: "with the head drawn back and the neck exposed to the sacrificial knife"). Hence the head of the shame-faced sinner is lifted up to bear the full brunt of God's gaze, God being the Judge to whom we shall have to give an account of our life here on earth. (Note that ". . . of Him with whom we have to do" is more literally: ". . . unto whom there is the account-rendering for us.")

E. The Superiority of the Son to Aaron as High Priest *(4:14-7:28)*.

(Note that the need of a priest has been suggested in the preceding section by the liability of believers to disobey and fail in faith. But the remedy for this frailty is not the summoning up of greater effort or intenser will-power, but in relying upon the Son as High Priest. In Him the feeblest of believers may confidently trust.)

1. **(4:14-16)** Since the Son is a priest wholly suited to our need, we may approach God through Him with complete confidence that we shall obtain the grace we need, when we need it.

   a. Why the Son is suited to our need: (i) (:14) He has perfect access; He has appeared before God Himself in glory to represent us, and not simply in the earthly Holy of holies. We may ever continue to claim Him as our representative before the Throne. (ii) (:15) Because He is perfectly willing to represent us, inasmuch as He feels sympathy for the weaknesses of His people. This sympathy is insured by the fact that in all respects He endured our mortal temptations, without of course yielding to them.

   b. **(:16)** Therefore since He is perfectly able and perfectly willing to intercede for us before the Father, we may with confidence and assurance come before God Himself directly (without the need of any saint or angel to serve as intercessor) and receive from Him: (i) mercy — forgiveness for sin repented of and confessed; and (ii) grace — power of triumph over temptation, and supply of every need of body, mind or soul. And this mercy and grace is instantly available, just when we need it, arriving at the opportune time (*eis eukairon boētheian* — unto opportune succor).

2. **(5:1-4)** The qualifications for a valid high-priesthood, as indicated by the Levitical priesthood which God ordained.

   a. **(5:1a)** He must be chosen from among those whom

he is to represent before God, i. e. he must be of the human race.

b. **(:1b)** He is appointed not to serve himself or to exploit his office to personal advantage, but to serve others, acting as their representative.

c. **(:1c)** His representation is to be made effective before God by the offering of sacrifices to atone for sin.

d. **(:2a)** His intercession must be expressed from his heart, a heart affected with a proper sympathy ("being able moderately to suffer" — *metriopathein* — rather than with an excessive or partisan sympathy which takes sides with sin as against holy justice) for those who have committed sins of "ignorance" (i. e. of thoughtlessness or carelessness, but not intended to renounce the sovereignty of God) and have wandered from the Lord. (Note that this term, "sins of ignorance," involved in the reference to "the ignorant," refers to the teaching of Num. 15:27-31, which distinguishes between sins committed *bishegagah,* "an inadvertant-going-astray," and sins committed "with a high hand," by which an offender blasphemes God and denies His Lordship. For the latter type of sin, no sacrifice is provided.)

e. **(:2b)** His sympathy arises from the fact that he too has experience of human frailty (and therefore also of the need of leaning on God for strength and cleansing) .

  (i)   **(:3)** But of course the Levitical priest not only has had experience of weakness, but has even yielded to temptation himself, and must therefore offer atonement for himself as well as his people. (Implication: the Levitical priesthood therefore has no inherent validity, since an effectual mediator would have to be without personal guilt; it only serves as a type in anticipation of a valid priesthood of the Messiah Himself, ordained after a different order.)

3. **(5:4)** Therefore the Levitical high priest could not choose himself for this office, but had to be chosen by God Himself, as Aaron was.

4. **(5:5-6)** The divine appointment of Christ:
   a. Christ fulfilled this requirement in that the Father

Himself chose Him; He did not take this responsibility to Himself on His own authority.

b. Proof that the Father did choose Him is found in Ps. 2:7, fulfilled when the Father spoke these same words from heaven by an audible voice (at Christ's baptism, and at the Mount of Transfiguration).

c. Proof is found again in Ps. 110:4, where the Father ordains the Son as Priest. But He specifies there that His priesthood is not after the Levitical order but after the order of Melchizedek. This difference in priestly order gives the key to the superiority of the Son to Aaron as High Priest.

5. **(5:7-10)** How the Son fulfilled His intercessory function as High Priest.

a. **(:7)** In the days of His "flesh" *(sarx)*, i. e. when subject to the general conditions of humiliation in this present life (this particularly points to the Agony in Gethsemane): He made a sacrificial offering of "prayers" *(deōseis* — definite requests arising from specific situations) to God and "supplications" *(hiketeriai* — entreaties by victims of overwhelming calamity) accomplished by the external posture and gestures of entreaty, by tears of greatest earnestness. (A much-discussed question: What did He pray for? Apparently, according to this verse, that He might be saved *out of* death *(ek thanatou),* that is, to bring Him safely out of death into Resurrection life. The "cup" (Mat. 26:39) was not removed from Him so far as the shameful death — shameful in that He was identified with sinful man — was concerned. Yet the basic intent of the prayer *was* granted: that the power of death might be overcome, as it most gloriously was overcome, by the Crucifixion and Resurrection.)

(Supplemental note: Delitzsch interprets the transaction as follows: "To save out of *sōzein ek* — could only refer to His deliverance from succumbing to death spiritually. Jesus shrank back from this death because it involved experiencing the wrath of God and conflict with all the powers of sin. The Father answered His prayer by compassing Him about with love in the very midst of His mortal agony, and translating Him through dying into a life of glory. He was heard then, not by deliverance from the necessity of dying, but by converting His physical death into a gate of Paradise, the cross of shame into a ladder to heaven. Though as Man, He had to taste of death, God loosed its pangs (Acts 2:24) to make them the birth-throes of an endless life. And after all, if He had not experienced the terrors of death Himself, He could not have become "in all points . . . like as we," and He would to that extent have been disqualified to represent us.)

b. **(5:7b)** His prayer was answered because "He feared," more literally: "as a result of His reverential-awe *(eulabeia)*." This term comes from the verb *eulabeomai*, "to take a good, careful hold of something," hence to act with caution and wariness, out of anxiety or fear, out of caution, circumspection and reverent regard for what is holy. Hence *eulabeia* implies a religious reverence for God, and an anxiety not to offend Him, which manifests itself in voluntary and humble submission to His will. (Marcus Dods remarks at this point: The true answer to Christ's reverent submission was to give Him the cup to drink, and thus accomplish through Him the faultless will of God. To have saved Him from experiencing death would not have answered the *eulabeia* of His prayer.)

c. **(5:8-9)** By His suffering as to the consequences of obeying God rather than man, the Son (who forebore to exercise His prerogatives as God the Son) learned the meaning of obedience in the face of persecution, a learning which could only come on the basis of actual experience, an experience of doing that from which one shrinks but does nonetheless, because he knows it is the right and loving thing to do. This experience, even though it did not increase or perfect the perfection of obedience already residing in His heart, was nevertheless needful to qualify the Son perfectly as our High Priest. (There is, after all, a difference between a willingness to obey and actually having performed the deed of obedience, even though the deed is but the child of the intention.)

d. **(5:10)** The successful accomplishment of His high priestly sacrifice meant eternal salvation for believers, and thus He fulfilled the type of Melchizedek, whose peculiar significance is soon to be explained. (But first an exhortation to firmness of faith is inserted, comprising the rest of Chapter Five and all of Chapter Six. With Chapter Seven, Melchizedek is to be fully discussed.)

6. **(5:11-6:20)** Therefore, having such a High Priest, Christians are to forsake all vacillation and backwardness, and lay hold of this firm assurance of salvation afforded them by His accomplished propitiation.

   a. **(5:11-14)** The readers are reproved for their spiritual backwardness.

      (i)   **(5:11)** Melchizedek is an important type of Christ which needs to be properly appreciated, but for backward, immature Christians who are dull of hearing, the explanation will be difficult.

      (ii)   **(5:12)** You readers have no excuse for being so immature; instead you ought to be able to teach others, for you have been Christians for a long time and have had Bible teaching all your life. As it is, you yourselves need to be taught again the basic principles *(stoikheia)* of Biblical Christianity ("the oracles of God") and to review again the elementary Gospel truths taught to new converts in communicants' classes. And yet with your background of spiritual education, you should be ready for solid food (i. e. the deeper meaning of living in Christ).

      (iii) **(5:13)** It is immature Christians, who are mere babes *(nēpioi)* in the Lord, who need to be fed milk, i. e. the basic doctrines of salvation by Grace through faith, on the basis of Christ's finished work. To them it is still mostly theory, and they have not yet experienced the transformation it works in the viewpoint and behavior of a sanctified believer.

      (iv) **(5:14)** But "full age" or mature *(teleioi* — those who have attained the goal or *telos* of physical and dispositional adulthood) Christians are supposed to have solid food, since they have developed a spiritual habit-pattern *(hexis)* which puts them in possession of trained faculties of soul ("exercised," *gegymnasmena* — trained like athletes competing for a prize), faculties equipped for the discernment of basic spiritual issues. Their evangelical intuition enables them immediately to distinguish between the false and the true, the Scriptural and the un-Scriptural.

b. **(6:1-8)** The need of advancing to maturer spiritual understanding.

(1) **(6:1-3)** The Apostle prefers in his teaching to go on to deeper matters of doctrine, not going over again the basic principles of salvation. Such basic principles are: (a) evangelical repentance, forsaking all attempt at self-justification on the basis of good works (here called "dead" works, because there is no Life behind them, and they do not emanate from the indwelling Spirit of Christ); (b) faith in Christ's atonement and God's gracious imputation of His righteousness to the believer; (c) the distinction between Christian baptism and the ritual washings and sprinklings of Judaism; (d) the first enduement of the new believer with the Holy Ghost through a prayer of faith accompanied by the imposition of hands, sc. at baptism; (e) the bodily Resurrection of Christ, as a seal of His victory over sin and death on their behalf, and as a guarantee of their resurrection in glory at the Second Coming, and finally as the power behind our Christian living, as united with the risen Christ; (f) the final Judgment of the living and the dead, when they shall be assigned to their eternal abode in heaven or hell (or possibly "eternal judgment" also implies the judgment of Christians as to heavenly rewards). But without discussing these elementary teachings, the Apostle purposes to go on to more advanced teaching, as God grants him ability to explain it to them.

(2) **(6:4-5)** This forbearing to discuss first principles is justified because those who have been taught them already, if they by any chance have rejected and betrayed them, cannot be spoken to with any good effect. If they have been presented with the one way of salvation and have rejected it, there remains no other way by which they may repent and get back to God. In other words, the attempt to drill into them what has once been nominally accepted but has afterwards been utterly adjured (so that they say, "O yes, I've heard all that be-

fore; I know it by heart") is as useless as planting seed on bare rock.

(a) Any who have received the Light and have turned their back upon it can hardly come back to it again, since they have once and for all rejected it. God Himself has no other appeal to resort to, if the Cross is not sufficient and is permanently and conclusively despised.

(b) (:4-5) God has already done His utmost for such reprobates; not only have they been exposed to the truth of the Gospel, but they have experienced ("tasted") something of the sweetness of inclusion in the fellowship of the Church, they have been honored by the experience of what the Holy Spirit can do through them as far as they go along with Him (note that mere "partakers," *metokhoi*, are different from those who are actually indwelt by Him), for Christ gives Himself to man just as far as man gives himself to Him. To this limited extent an unsaved man may "partake of" the Holy Spirit, e. g. Judas Iscariot, who like the other Disciples cast out demons and cleansed the lepers and healed the sick (Mt. 10:5-8). These apostates have been taught the way of salvation in all of its reasonableness and convincing power, and have witnessed the great change it makes in the lives of believers, and yet in the face of all this compelling evidence and personal experience have nevertheless slipped aside (*parapiptō*) and fallen away.

(c) (6:6) To depart from the faith after receiving such knowledge shows a deliberate purpose of will to deny the Lord and join with those who condemned Christ to death as an imposter and subjected Him to shameful maltreatment on Good Friday.

(d) (6:7-8) By this deliberate choice in the face of full knowledge, they reveal their nature as utterly and finally unresponsive to all the influences of the Holy Spirit. Thus they resemble soil that refuses to bear crops despite

40

a generous rainfall, and produces only weeds and thistles and trash fit only for burning. (Is. 55:10-11 shows how the rain upon the soil represents the operation of the Holy Spirit in applying the word of God to the dirty soil of the human heart, that it may bring forth the fruit of a godly life.)

c. **(6:9-12)** But you, my readers, are surely ready for this advanced teaching I am about to give you, and do not need to remain any longer in spiritual immaturity.

   (1) **(:9)** My description of these apostates does not imply that any of you are such, but simply shows that it is pointless for me to linger on basic salvation doctrines. Rather, I should confirm you in your sense of assurance in Christ, on the basis of God's assurances through the promises and types of the O. T.

   (2) **(6:10)** Your readiness to advance in knowledge is attested by your previous experience of the Lord, who gave you victory, the capacity to love and to bear fruit in service, upholding your fellow-Christians. God's covenant-faithfulness is the guarantee of your perseverance in the faith.

   (3) **(6:11)** By following this teaching you will avoid sluggishness in hearing and obeying God, but will on the other hand follow the example of the O. T. heroes of the faith, whom no pressure from the world or the powers of sin could tear away from their loyalty to God or discourage from a patient endurance of affliction. Without self-pity or complaint or rebelliousness towards God they endured whatever pressures or afflictions He permitted. Such loyalty and steadfast endurance is possible for you too, for you have inherited the gracious promises Jehovah bestowed upon Israel.

d. **(6:13-20)** Instead of feeble vacillation, you are entitled to unshakable firmness under the covenant promise of grace conferred upon Abraham (and to his spiritual descendants).

   (1) **(:14)** This covenant promise was guaranteed by God's solemn oath, for He said in Gen. 22:16: "I have sworn by Me."

41

(2) **(:15)** Resting on this promise despite all adverse appearances (for he was already ninety-nine, Sarah was long past change of life, and many years had elapsed since the first giving of the promise in Gen. 12:1-3), Abraham lived to see it fulfilled for him. Note that his resting upon the divine promise was demonstrated by his patient endurance and refusal to complain (implied by *makrothymēsas*, "having patiently endured").

(3) **(:13)** This oath represented the most reliable sort of promise that could possibly be made, since God staked His integrity and authority upon its fulfilment.

  (a) **(:16)** *A fortiori*, if an oath among men serves to settle a matter beyond any further dispute, much more an oath made by God Himself. (:17) And so God resorted to an oath to convey to Abraham and his spiritual descendants the absolute dependability of His gracious promise, because it will never be altered or set aside (*to ametatheton* — "the immutability" or "the unchangeableness").

e. **(6:18-20)** The firm assurance which this covenant promise conveys to us:

(1) The very integrity of the Almighty is involved in the fulfilment of this guarantee of blessing, since He has so wholly committed Himself to it.

(2) God's promise could never be broken, and His confirmatory oath could never fail of fulfilment, since it is impossible for God, who is the Truth and in whom is no darkness at all, to make a lying promise.

(3) These two things, then, the oath and the promise, provide a sure encouragement to those who have fled for refuge to Him (despairing of any salvation outside of Him, and knowing how they are pursued by the powers of hell). Note: those who flee to God do so to lay hold upon the hope or assurance of this covenant promise as a storm-tossed ship in need of an anchor.

(4) This anchor of the divine promise is safe because it has its holding-ground up in glory in the presence of God and in the person of the Son Himself.

(a) Being in the presence of God, the Son has penetrated through the barrier which separates a holy God from an unholy mankind, the barrier symbolized by the inner veil *(pārōkheth)* of the Tabernacle, which shut off the Ark from Israel.

(b) The Son, as our Representative, has entered the Holiest of all (i. e. the Sanctum in heaven itself) as the forerunner of all believers who are in Him by faith, and who are therefore no longer separated from Him by the barrier of sin and creatureliness.

(5) **(6:20)** By entering into God's presence the Son fulfilled the type of Melchizedek and fulfilled the promise of everlasting High Priesthood associated with Melchizedek's name in Ps. 110:4.

7. **(7:1-17)** How the High-Priesthood of Melchizedek's Order is Superior to that of Aaron.

a. **(7:1-3)** The historical record of Gen. 14 indicates that: (1) the name of the priest-king was Melchizedek, (2) he was King of Salem (i. e. Jerusalem), (3) he blessed Abraham when he returned in victory from battle (having overcome impossible odds in a work of rescue, the deliverance of Lot and his associates — a demonstration of God's ability to triumph over apparent impossibilities and overcome the mighty of this world by the work of the weak and foolish who trust in Him and act as His servants) and (4) to him Abraham gave a tithe of the booty he had taken in battle. The application, showing how Melchizedek typified Christ:

(i) His name itself meant "King of Righteousness" *(melekh* — "king," *sedeq* — "righteousness").

(ii) He was King of Salem, i. e. King of Peace; for name *Shālēm* means "peace," being a dialectical by-form of *Shālōm*, the customary Hebrew term for peace (cf. Is. 9:6, where the Messiah is entitled *Sar shālōm*, "Prince of peace").

(iii) In the Genesis account Melchizedek had no recorded parentage or posterity, and neither his birth nor his death is recorded. This passage does not imply that he historically possessed no parents and never experienced birth or death. It simply emphasizes that the Holy Spirit so guided Moses in omitting these details in the sacred record that these ordinarily included details are strikingly omitted, thus preserving Melchizedek as a type of the Messiah. On the other hand, the only other O. T. reference to him, Ps. 110:4, speaks of the Melchizedek high-priesthood as enduring forever, long after the historical personage himself had passed away.

b. **(7:4-10)** Further application (showing the superiority of the Melchizedek high-priesthood to the Aaronic) of the transaction whereby Abraham paid tithes to Melchizedek.

  (1) **(:5)** The Levitical (Aaronic) priests are supposed under the Law to receive tithes from the rest of the tribes of Israel, the descendants of Abraham.

  (2) **(:6)** But even though he had already received God's covenant promise of blessing, Abraham was led to pay tithes to this Melchizedek, who was not of his kindred at all. Moreover he received a priestly blessing from him.

  (3) **(:7)** But obviously it is only the superior who can validly bestow a blessing upon another, and such other must in some respect be his inferior. (Such was Abraham to this Messiah-typifying priest.)

  (4) **(:8)** Moreover, the Levitical priests are mortal, subject to death like other men, but according to Ps. 110:4, the Messianic High Priest of the order of Melchizedek is immortal, since he is spoken of as exercising his priesthood *forever* (*eis to aiōna*, corresponding to the Heb. *le'ōlām*).

  (5) **(:9-10)** Lastly, in conformity with (2) above, Levi and the Aaronic priesthood were inferior to Melchizedek, since through their ancestor Abraham they paid him tithes.

c. **(7:11-14)** The Melchizedek high-priesthood must have been necessary to accomplish what the Levitical high-priesthood could not, else God would not have seen fit to ordain it subsequently to the establishment of the priesthood of Aaron under the Mosaic Covenant (in Ps. 110:4).

  (1) There could have been no "perfection" (*teleiōsis*

44

— a perfect fulfilment and achievement of the ends for which the priesthood was set up), otherwise God would not have needed to establish this new, Melchizedek priesthood to perfect it.

(2) This new Ps. 110 ordinance concerning Melchizedek priesthood involved nothing less than a complete superseding of the Mosaic system and constitution, since the latter was altogether based upon a Levitical priesthood, so far as worship and sacrifice were concerned. If then the priesthood is to be changed, the entire Old Covenant system with its provisions for atonement and access to God must necessarily be superseded as well.

(3) That the Mosaic constitution has been supplanted by Christ and the New Covenant economy is also shown by the fact that the Savior Himself was not descended from Levi but from the non-priestly tribe of Judah. Therefore Jesus could not have been intended by God to carry on His high-priesthood within the limits of the O. T. dispensation. The Mosaic Law made no provision for any but a Levite to serve as a valid priest.

d. (7:15-17) Therefore the Melchizedek high-priesthood is superior to the Aaronic, because of the immortality of the Antitype, Jesus Christ.

(1) This new high-priesthood has clearly been ordained according to the power of indestructible *life* (*zōē*), not according to the Mosaic regulation which was adapted to mere mortal limitations, and presupposed a mere human priest, morally imperfect and physically subject to death, as a limitation upon his span of life.

(2) No other conclusion can be drawn from the significant term "forever," found in Ps. 110:4.

8. (7:18-22) The New Order resulting from the new Priesthood of the Melchizedek-type.

a. (7:18-20) Because the Aaronic priesthood was merely provisional and could not of itself accomplish the purposes of cleansing, forgiveness and sanctification which it was designed to cover, therefore it has been set aside in favor of a new priesthood which will actually achieve these ends, the priesthood of the Messiah.

(1) The Mosaic Law could not by itself make men perfect or prepared to receive God's redemption in all its fulness and final validity.

(2) But what the Melchizedek High-priesthood has accomplished affords us a better assurance of hope because Christ has, as our Representative, overpassed the sin-barrier with His sinlessness and entered into the very presence of God in order to receive for Christians the fulness of redeeming Grace.

b. **(7:21)** The Melchizedek priesthood of Christ is final and valid because God Himself undertook personally to guarantee its efficacy — by a solemn oath: "Jehovah has sworn and will not change His purpose: Thou art a Priest forever . . ." (Ps. 110:4).

(1) This establishes Messiah's priesthood as superior to that of Aaron, which, although ordained by God, was nevertheless guaranteed and supported by no such oath as this.

(2) Because of this divine oath, Christ as High Priest after the order of Melchizedek became guarantor of a New Covenant superior to the Old Covenant made with Israel at Sinai.

(a) As Guarantor or "Surety" *(engyos)* Christ secures this New Covenant as surely achieving its end. That is, He is surety for men to God (or possibly also for God to men).

(b) Note that the Biblical term Covenant *(diathēkē)* does not imply a compact between two parties who stand on an equal footing (which would in Greek be *synthēkē*), but rather a unilateral disposing of one's own property (usually by will) according to his own good pleasure. The parties involved in this disposition could accept or reject the provisions specified, but they were not at liberty to alter them in the slightest.

9. **(7:23-28)** The complete efficacy of the Melchizedek High Priesthood of the Messianic Son of God.

a. **(:23)** The Son, as Antitype of Melchizedek, possesses a priestly office which can never pass away, because He Himself lives on forever, never to be cut off by death.

46

The Aaronic priests, on the other hand, were of limited efficacy because of their limited lifespan; they had to succeed one another in order to keep the office filled.

b. **(:24)** Therefore Christ, and He alone, is qualified to save fully and completely those who come to God by Him, for His intercession cannot fail to be effectual on their behalf. Nor will His intercession ever cease, since He will never be cut off by death (as were Aaron and his successors).

c. **(:26)** That His intercession will be effectual is guaranteed by (i) His own perfect righteousness and holiness, (ii) His exaltation to the heavens, at the right hand of the Father (for this position at His right hand amounts to an unqualified affirmation of Christ's sinless perfection and complete fulfilment of the Moral Law).

d. **(:27-28)** His effectiveness in intercession is guaranteed also by the permanent sufficiency of His atoning sacrifice, as contrasted with the insufficiency of the Levitical sacrifices.

(1) The Aaronic priesthood had to offer sacrifice every day, whereas Christ's sacrifice was offered only once, i. e. the sacrifice of Himself upon the cross.

(2) Whereas the Aaronic priests had to sacrifice for their own sins, being mere mortals of moral weakness and imperfection, Jesus Christ was sinless and made perfect (both in His personal morality and as Substitute for sinful man) for all time to come.

(3) **(7:28b)** It should be remembered also that His priesthood, while resting on a type appearing before the Mosaic Law was given, was revealed long afterward in a Davidic Psalm, established by God's solemn oath. Therefore by God's own ordinance it was to supersede the Law.

II. SUPERIORITY OF THE NEW COVENANT (8:1-10:18)

A. The Evanescence of the Old Covenant *(8:1-13)*.

1. **(8:1-6)** The High Priestly work of the Son as establishing the New Covenant.

   a. **(:1-2)** Theme: Christ as minister of the true Tabernacle in heaven. Seated at the right hand of Power in heaven, this High Priest of ours serves as a minister *(leitourgos)* of the true heavenly Tabernacle, the archetype of the earthly Mosaic Tabernacle. (*Leitourgos* means literally "one who labors for the people," hence "a .public servant" or "minister of state"; then, in a religious sense, "one who labors for God in the public interest." It was often applied to the servants of priests, then to priests themselves as God's servants. The related noun *leitourgia*, "public service" has come into English as *liturgy*.)

   b. **(:3-13)** Christ's offerings and service were more excellent, fulfilling the promise of the New Covenant.

      (1) **(:3)** Priests have the duty of offering sacrifice; therefore He also has offered a sacrifice to the Father in heaven.

         (a) **(:4)** The only proper sphere for the exercising of Christ's priesthood is in the heavenly Sanctuary, inasmuch as on earth there already are (and still are — note this evidence that *Hebrews* was written before the fall of Jerusalem in 70 A.D.) earthly priests who offer sacrifices according to the Mosaic Law.

      (2) **(:5)** That there is a heavenly archetype of the Sanctuary is proved by Ex. 25:40: ". . . make it according to their pattern, which thou art beholding in the mountain." When God so directed Moses, He must have had a heavenly original in mind, in order for a pattern (Heb. *tabnīth*) to be possible. It follows that the Tabernacle of Moses was only a copy or model, lacking any final validity of its own.

      (3) **(:6)** It must be then that Christ has entered upon

49

a superior priestly service to that of Aaron, superior to the same degree that the New Covenant is superior to the Old.

2. **(8:7-13)** The superiority of the New Covenant ensues from the superior promises which it contains, and from God's plain declaration that it is to supersede the Old.

   a. **(:7)** The mere fact that a new covenant had to be entered into shows there was something vital lacking in the old covenant, something essential to the perfect accomplishment of the purposes for which the Covenant was given in the first place.

   b. **(:8-9)** This insufficiency of the Old Covenant was indicated by God's implied criticism of those who had entered into it with Him, when He said in Jer. 31:32, "Not according to the covenant which I made with their fathers . . . which covenant of Mine they themselves broke." There is no reason why God would not have kept the same covenant in force if it had been perfectly satisfactory. The covenant entered into at Sinai (Ex. 19:5-8) was of the tenderest, most fatherly sort (note that the Hebrew text of Jer. 31:32c says: "even though I Myself acted-as-husband toward them," rather than the Septuagint reading here quoted: "and I regarded them not"). Yet its purpose was frustrated because Israel chose to disobey, the Law not having taken lodgement in their heart.

   c. **(8:10a)** The superiority of the New Covenant is explained in Jer. 31:33 as consisting in this: that the holy Law will be implanted in the very hearts of God's people. (How? By the New Birth, which comes to pass when the Holy Spirit, whose will the Law expresses, takes up residence in the believer's soul. As possessed and indwelt by the Holy Spirit, the child of God under the New Covenant has a love for the Law, the love of the Holy Spirit Himself. He obeys the Law because he personally desires to, not because he feels constrained to by the pressure of fear or duty.)

   d. **(:10b-11a)** The result of this implanting: believers under the New Covenant will be in a fuller sense the holy people of God, and shall have personal, intimate knowledge of God. In a fuller sense He shall be *their* God, for they will enthrone Him in their hearts as the supreme Motive for all of life, and His Spirit will permanently abide within them (cf. John 14:17).

  e. **(:11b)** Equality of believers under the New Covenant: all classes and age-groups will enjoy this personal knowledge of God, and it will no longer have to be taught to them by human teachers as something alien to their nature, but rather it shall be part of their own experience.

  f. **(:12)** Under the New Covenant also the forgiveness of sins will be effectually bestowed (through the Substitutionary Atonement) and sins will be so canceled as to be completely deleted from the records.

  g. **(:13)** The New Covenant by its very designation as "new" makes the Old Covenant obsolescent and ready to pass away completely as something superseded.

B. The Spiritual Tabernacle and Sacrifice Superseding the Physical *(9:1-29)*.

  1. **(9:1-10)** Superiority of the heavenly Tabernacle to the earthly Tabernacle of the Old Covenant.

    a. **(9:1-5)** The contents of the earthly Tabernacle and the corresponding ordinances of worship.

      (1) The sacred furniture in the Holy Place (Heb. *qōdesh*): (i) the Candelabrum (which held the seven oil-lamps) (ii) the Table and the setting forth of the loaves (so the Greek, literally; corresponding to the Heb. *shulhān welehem pānīm,* or "the Table and the Bread of the Presence [sc. of God]").

      (2) The furniture in the Holiest Place ("Holy of holies," Heb. *qōdesh qodāshīm*) behind the impassable second veil: (i) at the very entrance (actually on the other side of the curtain or "veil") the golden altar of incense (the smoke of which floated up over the Ark inside the Holy of holies) (ii) the Ark of the Covenant, containing (a) the golden pot of manna, placed there for a memorial according to Ex. 16:33; (b) the rod of Aaron which miraculously budded forth blossoms, a testimonial that Levites only could serve as priests (Num. 17:10); (c) the two tablets of the Law (the Ten Commandments), which alone remained in the Ark after the period of the Judges (I Ki. 8:9); (d) the golden lid of the Ark was the

"Mercy Seat" or "Propitiatory" (*kappōreth*, related to the verb *kippēr*, "atone").

b. **(9:6-8)** Difficult entrance into the Holiest Place: whereas the Holy Place was entered daily by officiating priests, yet (1) the Holiest Place could be entered only once a year; (2) only the High Priest could enter that one time of the year, the Day of Atonement; (3) even the High Priest could not enter without bearing the blood of atonement to present to the Lord. (It should be noted that the blood which the High Priest brought in was that of a bullock for his own sin-offering, and the blood of a goat for the sin-offering of the nation Israel.)

c. **(9:8-10)** Significance of this difficulty of access. It indicated that the perfect and complete way of access into the (heavenly) Sanctuary was not provided under the Old Covenant, which was mere provisional and preparatory for the New Covenant.

(1) Just as the difficulty of access to God through the Old Covenant has endured up until now, so the external symbols of this barrier have endured in the Temple at Jerusalem up until now.

(2) That O. T. worship is imperfect of itself and mere preparatory to the real fulfilment in Christ because it consists in mere external, physical symbols: i. e. sacrifices which cannot (however much they may lay hold upon God's promise of forgiveness) truly cleanse the conscience of the offeror, so as to give him an assurance of being inwardly purified and truly brought into communion and peace with God.

(a) This system of ceremonial purification consisted in material offerings of food and drink laid upon the altar, and in ritual washings of the offeror in water, and likewise of the priests (who were required to wash at the Laver before entering the Holy Place).

(b) These ordinances affecting the physical side of man, primarily, were therefore imposed on a merely temporary basis until the time of Messianic rectification (*diorthōsis* — a term used of setting a fracture, repairing a road or house, and therefore in general of putting aright and bringing matters into a satisfactory state, even as Christ does to this sin-sick world at His First and Second Advents).

2. **(9:11-14)** Christ's service in the Heavenly Tabernacle.

a. Christ has come to us ministering an atonement which consists not in mere hope or promise, but in a redemption already accomplished (sc. by His Crucifixion). (Note that the earlier and better reading in the Greek manuscripts changes the "of good things to come" of the King James Version to "of good things which have come to pass" — *genomenōn* instead of *genēsomenōn*.)

b. As High Priest He serves in the Heavenly Tabernacle, which is of spiritual construction, and therefore surpasses the Mosaic Tabernacle to the extent that spirit surpasses the mere physical and temporal.

c. As High Priest He has entered to present a perfect and inherently sufficient sacrifice for sin.

   (1) The O. T. priest could only offer the blood of brute beasts, who are in and of themselves without moral significance.

   (2) But Christ as the God-Man and sinless Second Adam offers His own shed blood.

   (3) The O. T. priest had to enter the Holiest Place every year, but Christ had to enter the Heavenly Sanctuary but once, and that was sufficient.

   (4) The sacrifice of the O. T. priest had to be repeated yearly, and therefore was at best only temporary in its effectiveness; but Christ's sacrifice was once and for all presented on Calvary, and is eternal in its effectiveness.

d. **(9:13-14)** *A fortiori,* the cleansing efficacy of Christ's blood is perfect, in contrast to the imperfection of animal sacrifices.

   (1) Under the Old Covenant, God extended ceremonial purity to those who, being defiled or unclean, came to Him through a high priest on the Day of Atonement, presenting for atonement the blood of sacrificed beasts, or who were sprinkled with holy water (mingled with the ashes of a sacrificed red heifer according to Num. 19).

   (2) But now under the New Covenant, it is the blood

of the Son of God which is presented for atonement. This cannot but be of greater potency to effectuate atonement because: (i) it was voluntary on His part, not involuntary as it was with sacrificial beasts (ii) it was rational, not animal (iii) it was spontaneous, rather than being prescribed by any express command of God (iv) it was moral, being a choice of will in order to glorify God in the salvation of sinners.

(3) **(9:14b)** It was through the Holy Spirit that Christ offered His atoning blood; i. e., His divine nature remained inseparable from Him and unchangeable, even in Crucifixion and death of His human body, so that He was the Priest offering Himself as victim. Moreover, it was Christ's Holy Spirit which prompted His sacrifice (in contrast with the involuntary sacrifice of beasts) and gave it efficacy. Thus the sacrifice belonged to the sphere of spiritual and eternal things, for the Spirit, being eternal, can alone be efficacious in eternal things.

(4) **(:14c)** Note also that the sacrifice of Christ not only atones for the guilty in a *forensic* way (i. e. by way of legal imputation, reckoning the righteousness and penal death of the Sin-bearer to those for whom He died), but it also produces an internal effect within the believer. That is, it cleanses his conscience from the pollution of "dead works," or the activity (whether self-justifying or self-seeking) of the unregenerate soul, "dead in trespasses and sins" (Eph. 2:1). Only deeds which are done by a born-again believer as a man *in* Christ, the Life, can be said to be *living* works; they are living works because Christ is expressing His life through His instrument (Rom. 6:13), the yielded body and soul of the yielded Christian. The result of this cleansing of the Christian's conscience is a new capacity to serve God acceptably, with a single eye to God's glory, apart from any self-interest or self-seeking.

3. **(9:15-28)** The better Covenant and the better Sacrifice.

a. **(:15)** Christ has therefore become Mediator of a better covenant, the New Covenant entered into upon the basis of His atoning death, rather than the death of mere brute beasts.

    (1) This New Covenant is distinguished from the Old in that it is based on a fulfilment of the promise of redemption from sin, i. e. upon the accomplished transaction whereby a life was given to satisfy the just demand of the broken Law (Ez. 18:20).

    (2) Because the transaction is accomplished, believers (i. e. those sinners who are called by God to partake of the everlasting inheritance of salvation) receive now a promise already fulfilled, not simply a hope of its eventual fulfilment (which was all the O. T. believers had). (Note: the blood sacrifices of the O. T. stood in the same relation to Christ's Atonement as a bank check bears to the actual payment in cash of the sum it specifies. The check is good, provided the payment is made; it is by itself only a worthless scrap of paper, but if it is supported by a corresponding deposit of good money in the bank, and the amount is actually honored in cash, the check turns out to be as good as gold. Every animal sacrifice under the Mosaic Law was a check drawn upon the atoning value of Christ's shed blood on Calvary.)

b. **(:16-17)** The New Covenant or Testament validated by the death of the Maker. (At this point review the definition of *diathēkē* given at 7:21 under b. (2) (b). *Diathēkē* is an almost unilateral type of covenant which involves a disposing of one's own property according to one's own good pleasure. Usually this Greek word means a *will* or *testament*, and hence it is appropriate to point out that this particular covenant resembles the operation of a will in that a death was necessary to validate it.) Note that under O. T. practice, and under ancient practice generally, it was customary to solemnize covenants or contracts by the offering of an animal sacrifice, which would of course involve validation by a death.

c. **(9:18-22)** The Old Covenant itself was ratified on the basis of the shed blood of a victim, according to Ex. 24:3-8, where we read

(1) that the terms of the basic moral law (Ex. 21-23) were fully declared to Israel, and the people accepted them;

(2) that the altar was then built with twelve boundary stones, representing the Twelve Tribes, surrounding it;

(3) that young men officiating as priests (since this was prior to the setting up of the Levitical priesthood) were commissioned to offer up bullocks as burnt offerings and peace offerings;

(4) that the blood was then divided into two parts, one half being sprinkled by Moses upon the altar itself, and the other half being caught in large, deep two-handled bowls *(aggānōth)*;

(5) that from these Moses sprinkled the elders and leaders representing the Twelve Tribes.

(6) Here the Apostle adds the information (not detailed in Ex. 24) that goat's blood was used as well as bull's blood; that scarlet wool and hyssop were used to do the sprinkling; that water was used as well as blood (cf. Lev. 14:5, where the two are used together in the cleansing of lepers) ; that the Book of the Covenant (Ex. 21-23) was sprinkled as well as the people themselves.

(7) Ex. 24:8 relates that Moses accompanied this sprinkling by the words: "Behold, the blood of the Covenant which Jehovah has made with you upon the basis of all these words" (so the Hebrew, literally) , which demonstrates the close connection between the Covenant and its validation by the shedding of blood.

(8) **(9:21)** Even the holy objects in the Tabernacle and the Tabernacle itself were ceremonially purified by the sprinkling with atoning blood. Of course this came later, after the Tabernacle had been erected. In Lev. 8:15 at the consecration service of Aaron, the altar was anointed with the blood of the sin-offering bullock. In Lev. 16:14 Aaron followed Moses' instructions to sprinkle the Mercy-seat with the blood of the bull and goat of the sin-offerings.

(9) **(9:22)** All of these regulations observed by Moses

and Aaron establish and illustrate the principle that nearly all things acceptable to God must be sanctified and atoned for by the shed blood of a sacrifice, and that sins under the Old Covenant were never forgiven without the death of an innocent victim.

d. **(9:23-28)** The once-and-for-all efficacy of Christ's single act of atonement. Just like the Old Covenant, so also the New had to be validated by the shedding of blood.

(1) **(:23)** The fact that the earthly types of the heavenly realities had to be atoned for shows that the heavenly originals themselves needed purification by a blood sacrifice (since it was for sinful men that the High Priest entered heaven) but of course by a sacrifice having validity for heaven and appropriate to heaven, rather than a mere animal sacrifice.

(2) **(:24)** Instead of entering into a mere earthly sanctuary fashioned by men (and therefore temporary), as Aaron did, Jesus has entered to minister as High Priest in heaven itself.

(a) Therefore He has come to intercede and present atonement not merely in the symbolic presence of God (as Aaron did in the Holiest Place), but into the actual presence of God up in heaven.

(3) **(:25)** Instead of being required to enter again and again, year by year, to present the atonement (as did the Levitical priest), Christ has entered God's true presence once and for all.

(a) Moreover He entered not to present the blood of some other creature (as Aaron did), but to present His own blood.

(4) **(:26a)** The fact that He has entered once and for all shows that His sacrifice has availed by itself, and without any need of its being repeated (as the Mass presupposes), to cancel out the sins of believers once and for all.

(5) **(:26b-27)** The one offering up of Himself in death corresponds to the fact that the people He represented on the Cross have themselves but one

death to die, at least one death prior to the final judgment of their souls before God. Just as man dies once and for all, so his Representative died once and for all.

(6) **(:28a)** This death of Christ constituted fulfilment of the prophecy of Is. 53:12: "And He Himself bore the sin of many."

(7) **(:28b)** That this sacrifice has been accepted by God as completely effectual as a once-and-for-all transaction is going to be confirmed some day by Christ's Second Coming in glory.

   (a) That which is the execution of a sentence of condemnation in the case of guilty mankind (i. e. physical death) will then be apparent as a deliverance ("salvation" — *sōtēria*), a gateway into heaven's glory. (Note that *sōtēria* here is used of the redemption of the believer's *body* at the Final Resurrection.)

   (b) But note that the return of the High Priest from His ministry beyond the veil (that is the heavenly Holy of Holies) will bring salvation to only one class of people: believers — here described as those who eagerly and expectantly wait *(apekdekhomai)* for Him (even as the Israelite congregation anxiously awaited the reappearance of the High Priest from the Holy of Holies on Yom Kippur).

C. The Superiority and Finality of the New Covenant *(10:1-18)*.

   1. **(10:1-4)** The Old Covenant afforded cleansing which was merely symbolic or provisional.

   (The Mosaic Law provided in its sacrificial system a mere shadowy representation of the Atonement which was later to take place — render "of the things" in v. 1 as "of the realities," *tōn pragmatōn;* it did not provide the actual substance of the redemptive transaction performed on Golgotha. It was, then, the sacrificial deed of Christ as the God-Man which provided the substantial form, "the very image" — *autēn tēn eikona,* a phrase in which *eikōn* means "that which is in itself substantial and gives a *true representation* of what it images, bringing before us, under conditions of space and time, that which is essentially spiritual in such a way as to be comprehensible to us in this life.")

58

a. The mere symbolic value of the Law and its sacrifices is shown up by the fact that the Aaronic priest had to repeat the same sacrifices year after year.

b. The need of repeating these offerings demonstrates that they did not make the offerors perfect *(teleioō),* i. e. did not cause them to attain fully unto the goal or purpose *(telos)* of their approach to God. (Cf. Westcott's comment here: "He who is *teleios* has reached the *end* which is in each case set before him: maturity of growth, complete development of powers, full enjoyment of privileges, perfect possession of knowledge.")

c. For had these O. T. offerings made the offerors "perfect," they would have ceased to offer them any longer, for then their conscience would have become clear and unburdened, had they been once and for all cleansed by such sacrifices.

d. But as it was, the Day of Atonement sacrifice testified to a recollection of sin unatoned for.

e. Therefore it necessarily follows that the mere blood of animal sacrifices could not actually atone for and cancel out the sins of believers under the O. T. economy.

2. **(10:5-9)** The effectual and fulfilling nature of the sacrifice of Christ's body. (The O. T. itself testifies that the animal sacrifices were not the ultimate remedy of God for man's sin, but simply provisional for the sustaining and nourishing of faith in a coming Atonement that *would* be effectual.)

a. **(:5-6)** This is proven by Ps. 40:7-9, in which David speaks of his Messianic Antitype and is guided by the Holy Spirit into a phaseology particularly appropriate for the Messiah when He comes into the world as God in human flesh. (Note that not all of Ps. 40 can be considered as Messianic, since in v. 12 David confesses he has been guilty of innumerable sins. In that passage he speaks personally and not typically.)

(1) Messianic David there avers that offerings of animals and of grain *(thysia* and *prosphora)* were not the essential requirements of God, but only as a sign and evidence of an obedient and yielded heart in the worshipper himself.

(2) Note that the Heb. original, "ears hast Thou pierced for Me," stresses the ear as that organ of

man which hearkens to God's word for the purpose of obeying it; the paraphrase of the Greek Septuagint (which the Apostle partially follows here) puts it: "ears hast Thou *prepared* for Me"; but the Apostle enlarges the concept here, making explicit what was clearly implied by the Heb., saying: "a *body* hast Thou *prepared* for Me." Note that the piercing of the ear was under Mosaic Law a rite which made a voluntary slave into a lifelong possession of his beloved master (Ex. 21:6). Thus the piercing of the ear was equivalent to preparing the whole body or person of the slave for lifelong service.

(3) Recognizing the requirement of obedience to God's revealed will as the prime essential for pleasing the holy God, Messianic David resolves to enter into the kingship to which God had summoned him. (Historically this refers to God's summons to David from Ziklag in the Philistine territory, for this Psalm was probably written about the time of Saul's death at the Battle of Mt. Gilboa.)

b. **(10:7)** The antitypical Messiah surrenders His will wholly to do the will of God. Specifically, this refers to Deut. 19 where the Lord predicts that there will be a king over Israel (just as in Deut. 18 He had indicated that a great Prophet like Moses would be given the nation). David here yields himself to fulfil the duties of the King of Israel under the Covenant, and to do so with obedience unreserved. More generally speaking, the Messiah finds the Scripture filled with references to Himself as Prophet, Priest and King, and He has come into the world for the express purpose of doing the will of His Father above every other consideration or desire.

c. **(10:8-9)** If, then, the Levitical sacrifices are subordinated to the obedient performance of God's will (by the one Person who was morally and spiritually qualified to perform it), then the Old Covenant must necessarily be abolished in order that the New Covenant may be established in its place.

3. **(10:10-13)** The permanent effectiveness of Christ's sacrifice results in the finality of His triumph.

a. **(:10)** Therefore this offering up of an obedient life by the Messiah results in the once-and-for-all cleansing and sanctifying of all those for whom the Messiah suffered as their representative.

b. **(:11-12a)** Contrast the ineffectiveness of Levitical sacrifices under the Old Covenant — which had to be repeated daily and which did not actually remove sins — and the sacrifice of Christ Himself, which by its non-repetition exhibited a real effectiveness to perform a perfect atonement.

c. **(:12b-13)** The sufficiency and finality of this sacrifice led to the exaltation of Christ to the place of supreme glory and authority over God's universe, so that all things are subject to His rule (as predicted in Ps. 110:1). This supremacy will inevitably (because of God's decree) lead to an ultimate complete vanquishing of all who oppose Christ.

4. **(10:14-18)** The Atonement works a complete transformation of the inner nature of believers.

a. **(:14)** The single sacrifice of Christ's body upon the cross brings to pass a complete cleansing and hallowing of believers, a rendering holy or sanctifying which shall remain permanently effectual.

b. **(:15-17)** This results in a transformation of the inner nature of the believer (as well as rendering him judicially acquitted before the Law), for Jer. 31:33 so states (after announcing the New Covenant):

  (1) The Law of God, or His principles for holy living, will no longer come to the believer as something imposed from without, but shall be placed in the heart or inner nature of the child of God. Because they are in his heart, he will spontaneously love them and prefer to follow them, as well as approving and embracing them in his mind as matters of moral conviction.

  (2) **(:17)** This inward change of attitude will be accompanied by so complete a forgiveness of the sins of believers under the New Covenant that they will not even be remembered (i. e. registered in heaven's record-books) any more.

  (3) **(:18)** Because of the full and final nature of the forgiveness of sins under the New Covenant, there

61

is no longer any sacrifice that needs to be offered (not even any "repetition of the sacrifice of Calvary" such as the Roman "priests" pretend to perform at the sacrament of Holy Communion).

III. SUPERIOR RESOURCES FOR VICTORIOUS FAITH
(10:19-13:25)

A. Encouragement to Hold Firm and Use the New Access to God *(10:19-39)*

   1. **(10:19-21)** The superior privileges of access to God resulting from removal of barriers by the Messianic High Priest.

      a. **(:19)** We have the right to enter freely into the Holy of Holies (i. e. the spiritual antitype, the presence of Almighty God), a right which arises from the sacrifice of Christ's life for us (in His shed blood).

      b. **(:20a)** This right of entering in before God comes to believers as a fresh way of access, depending not upon the sacrifice of mere animals, but rather upon the accomplished atonement of the Son of God Himself.

      c. **(:20b)** Entering in before God in the Holy of Holies meant passing through the second veil (the *pārōkheth*), a curtain which symbolized the barrier of human nature ("flesh," *sarx*, the fallen nature of Adam, as dwelling in a weak and temptable body); but Christ, assuming that "flesh" or human nature, and giving up His body to be torn and pierced in the Crucifixion, by this means effectuated a rending apart of the Second Veil which separated believers from their God. Thus He disposed of the barrier of the Adamic nature and opened up free entrance for us into God's presence.

      d. **(:21)** We now have access through a High Priest who has entered once and for all into God's actual presence to represent our cause and secure salvation for us.

   2. **(10:22)** Resultant freedom of access may be and should be used unhesitatingly by believers, i. e. as those who are cleansed and sanctified by God.

      a. They are to keep coming (note the present subjunctive form) with a sincere, God-surrendered heart.

      b. They are to come with a faith confident and unreserved, taking God at His word.

      c. They are to come with hearts cleansed of the self-seeking principle of sin, and cleansed of all sense of continuing guilt, since the guilt has already been atoned for.

d. They are to come with cleansed bodies, that is, with bodies rendered holy, separated from bondage unto self-seeking lusts and set apart for service of the Lord in His sanctuary, i. e. in the work of the Kingdom. In this connection, note that "pure water" refers to the sacrament of baptism; the water of baptism is a sort of antitype of the "holy water" of Num. 5:17. Compare Ez. 36:25, which predicts that believers who shall be indwelt by God's Spirit and inwardly transformed will be sprinkled with "pure water."

3. **(10:23)** The reason for keeping firm hold of the affirmation, "I know I am saved," and for maintaining this confidence of acquittal at the Last Judgment and of sharing in the glory of Christ's return:

a. Trustworthy and dependable is the God who promised that those who have received Christ are saved and adopted into His holy family.

b. All this is implied by *homologian tēs elpidos*, "profession of hope," rather misleadingly translated by "the profession of our *faith*." Here the *homologia* or "profession" may be also rendered "confession," and implies such an affirmation as this: "I affirm *(homologeō)* with God that I am a lost sinner, justified only by Grace through faith, and that I shall be openly acknowledged and acquitted by God at the Last Judgment, when Jesus comes as King to rule over the world." It is the latter part of the statement which especially pertains to the *tēs elpidos*, "of hope," more accurately: "of confident expectation."

4. **(10:24-25)** Result of retaining this profession of hope: the encouragement of brother Christians in lives of fruitful service.

a. **(:24a)** "Let us consider" is *katnoōmen* (which implies: "Let us constantly direct our mind intensively towards") , i. e. we are to achieve an intelligent insight into the problems and spiritual needs of our fellow-Christians. Hence the exhortation to consider attentively our neighbor's circumstances and situation, not with a view to criticism but with a view to encouragement and help.

b. **(:24b)** As we encourage our brethren, our purpose is to spur them on to realize the mighty potentialities within them and allow the love of the indwelling Christ to work through them His own fruitful works of redemption, healing and comfort. (It is only He who can perform genuinely *good* works, but He is pleased to work them through us.)

c. **(:25a)** In the interests of this encouragement the believer will frequent the meetings for testimony and prayer in fellowship with his church, rather than following the evil example of some professing believers who (even in that day!) forsook church-attendance, thus leaving his fellow-Christians in the lurch (such is the force of the verb "forsaking" — *enkataleipō*) and affording them no encouragement at all in their battle of faith.

d. **(:25b)** In contrast to this neglect of church, the true believer is to be faithfully on hand for the exhortation of his brethren in the work of the Lord (a somewhat higher and more positive purpose than that which motivates the average church-goer), and that too with a spirit of real urgency and earnestness in view of the approach of the Day of Christ.

    (1) In this connection note that the signs which are to precede the final Battle of Armageddon are very similar to those which preceded the First Jewish Revolt and the Fall of Jerusalem to Titus in 70 A.D. So much is this the case that one report of Christ's Olivet Discourse, that of Luke in his twenty-first chapter, is felt by many expositors to apply only to that Roman siege, even though the parallels in Matthew and Luke take in the catastrophic events of the End Time.

    (2) Note also that the approach of Christ's judgment upon apostate Jewry in 70 A.D. was to terminate completely and forever the obsolete Temple worship which perpetuated typical rites fulfilled by the Crucifixion. Just as Jehovah in the O. T. is often spoken of as returning to His people when He visited them with either deliverance or chastening judgments, so here (according to the familiar Hebrew mode of expression) Christ returned (to

punish) when Jerusalem fell to the Roman legions. In this sense the Apostles were not mistaken when they looked forward to a speedy return of the Lord (Rom. 13:12; Phil. 4:5; Jas. 5:8; I Pet. 4:7), even though they may not have been completely aware of the fact that the coming catastrophe of 70 A.D. would in turn prefigure a second catastrophe, or near-catastrophe, which would truly consummate the final judgments of the Day of the Lord. In other words, the encompassing of Jerusalem with armies which occurred in the Apostolic Age was but a prophetic event pointing forward to the eschatological encompassing of Jerusalem with armies (also embraced in the purview of the Olivet Discourse).

5. **(10:26-39)** The surpassing guilt of those who spurn this Christ-prepared Access to God: an exhortation to constancy.

   a. **(:26-31)** The hopeless condition of those who reject the Cross, God's utmost for their redemption.

      (1) **(:26)** If professing believers go on wilfully in sin (the present participle *hamartanontōn* implies: "As long as we are wilfully sinning"), indulging it in such a way as virtually to deny that Christ is their Lord, even after they have received a valid intellectual understanding *(epignōsis)* of the Gospel-truth, then they are guilty of a deliberate rejection of all God did on Calvary. But the Cross was the utmost God could possibly do to save men from their sin and from the condemnation of hell.

      (2) **(:27)** The only possible alternative, in view of this wilful persistence in sin, is a terrible condemnation reserved for all who fight on Satan's side ("the adversaries") against God. What other alternative is left for God but the punishing fires of hell?

      (3) **(:28-29)** *A fortiori*, since the Israelite under the Old Covenant who was convicted of rejecting the authority of the Mosaic Law was surely put to death (after he had been adjudged guilty through the testimony of two or more witnesses — cf. Deut. 17:6) without possibility of pardon, therefore the

rejection of Christ and His Gospel warrants punishment, and that too of far greater severity than physical death. For rejecting the N. T. Gospel after making a profession of Christ is tantamount to:

   (a) trampling contemptuously upon the Son of God,

   (b) deeming unholy and worthless the blood which He shed to validate the New Covenant, and

   (c) committing outrage or casting insult upon *(enhybrisas)* the gracious Holy Spirit.

(It would seem to follow that if this is no true picture of the inner attitude of the backslider, but rather it remains true that in his heart he really means to honor Christ as his Lord and to count His blood precious and to revere His Spirit, then he does not fall into the class of hopeless apostates of whom the Scripture speaks in this passage. Nevertheless there is a solemn warning here that trifling with the Lord can lead to such a hardening of heart that the backslider becomes a true apostate who no longer has any care about his soul.)

(4) **(:30-31)** God's faithfulness in upholding the Moral Law means the inevitable doom of apostates who trample on it.

   (a) Proved by Deut. 32:35, which teaches that retribution and reward are the special prerogatives of God the Judge.

   (b) Proved by Ps. 135:14, which guarantees that God will judge even His own people, Israel, and not permit them to go on indefinitely in self-will and infidelity. No matter how much He loves His covenant-children, He must out of love to His moral universe and to the highest interests of all His creation prevent the incorrigible and wilfully disobedient from working irreparable harm to the rest of His creatures. This He can do only by imposing the dread penalties of His Law, which is spoken of here as "falling into His hands."

b. **(10:32-35)** Exhortation to firmness of faith in view of the past temptations which they have triumphantly endured.

(1) **(:32)** The glory of the victories achieved in the bloom of the early days of their new life soon after conversion is brought to their mind. They triumphed over temptation (here spoken of as *athlēsis,* "the struggle of an athlete".) like contestants who win a crown. (*Athlēsis* is rendered "fight" in the KJV.)

(2) **(:33-34)** The various forms of the temptation: (a) ridicule by the world as they were exposed to public contempt and shame like victims in an arena or theatre *(theatrizomenoi),* being reviled and scorned by their own compatriots (as converts to Protestantism in Latin America are often vilified by their unconverted fellow-citizens or relatives) ; (b) subjection to pressure of a physical or economic nature ("the spoiling of your goods") brought on by the ill-will borne them by the public because of their new faith; (c) suffering the unpopularity of being linked with those like Peter and Paul and Timothy who were imprisoned and prosecuted as disreputable criminals.

Their response to these testings: they willingly became "companions" or sharers *(koinōnoi)* of those Christians who were thus publicly persecuted and disgraced; they endured the loss of property, not simply with uncomplaining resignation but with a sense of joy that they were accounted worthy to suffer shame for Christ's name, and buoyed up by the conviction that they had in Him a far more precious possession than any of this world's goods, a treasure which time could never take away. (Note: when a Christian has a chance to behave in the opposite fashion from what a worldling would do in the same circumstances, that is a shining-time for the Lord Jesus.)

(3) **(:35a)** Having thus gloriously tasted the sweetness of triumph over the pressures of the Christ-opposing world, the Hebrew Christians must not now throw away their confident assurance which has been sealed by such confirming experiences. (The word "confidence" here is *parrēsia,* which means originally "freedom of speech," then "boldness or assurance of utterance"; hence a readiness

to proclaim before all the ground of hope upon
which the believer rests, as one who is sure of
victory — in the Lord.)

c. **(10:35b-39)** Exhortation to firmness in view of the
heavenly reward which lies ahead.

(1) **(:35b)** This confident assurance is directed towards a great reward which far outweighs any
afflictions the faithful may be called upon to
endure in this life.

(2) **(:36)** But this promised reward is bestowed only
upon those who have patiently endured to the end
in putting first the will of God. (Patience here is
hypomonē, which literally means a remaining
under the load, rather than impatiently seeking to
cast it off and escape from responsibility.)

(3) **(:37)** The nature of this reward is summed up in
the O. T. guarantee that Christ will come again
for His own and establish His rightful rule over
all the earth, in accordance with the promise of
Hab. 2:3 "For He shall surely come and will not
delay" (so the Heb.) .

(4) **(:38)** But what immediately follows in this
Habakkuk passage shows that the Second Advent
reward pertains only to those who have remained
steadfast in the faith: "My righteous one shall live
on the basis of faith (the Heb. puts it: "by his
faithfulness" — a meaning which the Greek *pistis,*
"faith," may also bear) ; and if he draws back
hesitantly, My soul takes no pleasure in him."
(The Heb. text as preserved to us shows minor
divergences from this Greek rendering: "Behold
his soul has become heedless (and) is not pleasing
within him; but a righteous one shall live by his
faithfulness." The KJV translates "become heedless" (*'uppelah)* as "which is lifted up," but the
meaning is uncertain either way, since the word
occurs only there in that conjugation. The Heb.
text preserved to us has "his soul" instead of the
"my soul" in the Greek; but the difference between
the two in the Heb. consonantal text is very slight,
and the final *y* could easily be confused with a
final *w,* or *vice versa.* KJV's "is not upright" is
literally correct for Heb. *yāsherah,* but often this

verb is used to convey the idea of conforming to or pleasing the standard or desire of someone; therefore if we read "My soul" instead of "his soul," the context calls for "be conformable to the standard or desire of" the Lord).

   (5) **(:39)** But true believers, who take their stand with the Apostle himself, are not guilty of such drawing back from a sincere and out-and-out faith, but cherish a steady and unshakable conviction which insures their obtaining the salvation of their soul.

B. The Power of an Overcoming Faith like that of the Heroes of the Old Testament *(Ch. 11)*.

   1. **(11:1-3)** The nature of true faith: trust in the unseen God and in His as yet unfulfilled promises.

     a. **(:1)** Faith is directed towards the unseen, that which has not yet been visibly proved and yet which is believed in with a firm assurance.

       (1) It is a "substance," or more accurately, "firm assurance" or "conviction" (*hypostasis* — a "standing under" something so as to support it with earnest conviction; some scholars interpret *hypostasis* here as a "title-deed," just as a deed guarantees ownership of a plot of real estate, since the word was so used in legal circles back in Apostolic times). And so faith is a firm assurance of things hoped for.

       (2) Faith is an "evidence," or better, "a proof or test" (*elenkhos*) of things or *realities (pragmata)* not seen. It is a demonstration of the solid truth of the tenets of the religion revealed by God.

       (3) It was needful to make this point clear at this particular juncture, in view of the complaint of the faint-hearted among the Hebrew Christians (implied in Chap. 10) that it was hard to wait and remain true in the face of the contempt of unconverted Jews and the ridicule of materialistic unbelievers who claimed to have the backing of solid realities. It was necessary to show that inherent in the very nature of faith is the reposing of confidence in realities unseen as yet, though some day to break into the visible realm with the Second Coming of the all-conquering Christ and the establishment of Heaven's rule upon earth ("of things hoped for" or "things confidently expected"

—elpizomenōn). If, then, faith has by definition to do with things not seen, the faithful believer must make no complaint on the ground that what he believes in has not been made visible, that is, brought into such three-dimensional reality as to convince every observer, even the materialist and the scoffing cynic. Therefore there is no basis whatever for bitterness if evil temporarily triumphs in this present age, for if it did not do so, and if the Gospel promises did not seem to conflict with external appearances, then there would be no occasion for faith to be called into play. And without faith how could there be salvation?

b. **(:2)** Mention of faith in the unseen, in promises of God as yet unfulfilled, is precisely the kind of faith exhibited by our spiritual forebears in the covenant family: the heroes in O. T. times, who are shortly to be enumerated.

c. **(:3)** This faith in the unseen must not be misunderstood as anti-rational or unreasonable, but rather it furnishes the necessary starting point for any coherent understanding of the visible world about us, for:

    (1) The visible, three-dimensional world must have been created out of nothing, if ever it had a beginning; and it must have been created by a Prime Mover, a First Cause, that is, by God's command.

    (2) Therefore the basis of the material universe must lie in the immaterial. (Observe how strikingly this statement anticipates the discovery of modern nuclear physics, that behind the most elemental constituents of matter is non-material whirling energy.)

2. **(11:4-7)** Faith as exhibited in the earliest of the saints: the Antediluvian Patriarchs.

a. **(:4)** Abel the Martyr: faith as recognizing the natural obligations of man to God and fulfilling them even unto death.

    (1) By the act of faith Abel offered a more abundant (rather than "excellent") sacrifice to God than did his brother Cain: more abundant because he offered himself with it, on the principle that, "All I have is God's," rather than Cain's "How much does God require?"

71

(2) Because of this faith Abel was accepted by God as righteous (as well as because his blood-sacrifice conformed to the Atonement on Calvary, whereas Cain's bloodless sacrifice did not).

(3) Being justified by God, Abel lives on and exerts an influence upon those who come after him in the procession of believers, and not simply as a matter of accusation against his brother before God ("The voice of thy brother cries out to me from the ground" — Gen. 4:10).

b. (:5-6) Enoch the Immortalized, who achieved a living fellowship with God.

(1) He never experienced physical death, for Gen. 5:24 implies that after his miraculous disappearance, his body was never found. This implies that he was accepted of God in a special way.

(2) The cause for this special exemption and privilege is found in the record that he *walked with* God, a statement which implies the closest intimacy and uninterrupted communion. Rather than render this idiom literally, the Greek Septuagint paraphrased by putting it, "Enoch pleased God"; it is this statement which the Apostle repeats here, doubtless because walking with God implies also pleasing Him. (Only while Adam pleased God did he have the privilege of walking with Him in the cool of the evening.)

(3) The fact that Enoch pleased God testifies to the fact that he lived a life of faith.

(a) This necessarily follows, since no one can possibly please God unless he has faith.

(b) Why is this so? Because God can only be pleased with one who approaches Him to worship, serve or hold communion with Him. (Cf. Zeph. 3:2: " (Jerusalem) trusted not in Jehovah, she did not *draw near* to her God" — no faith, no approach!)

(c) But no one can approach God unless he believes He is there to approach; he must believe that God is a real Person.

(d) Nor can he approach God unless he believes it is worth while to approach Him, in that He is a moral God who rewards those who earnestly and honestly seek Him, i. e. seek to know Him and please Him.

c. (:7) Noah the Righteous, who obeyed God and believed Him when He predicted the impossible.

   (1) It was enough for Noah that God had told him the Flood was coming; he took Him at His word.

   (2) (first test of faith:) even though no such flood had ever yet occurred, certainly none great enough to destroy all life;

   (3) (second test of faith:) and he engaged in an enormous construction project, because God told him to, even though building a huge ship on dry land exposed him to the ridicule of all his neighbors.

   (4) His personal reward: the deliverance of himself and his entire family from the otherwise universal destruction.

   (5) His personal privilege: a good testimony for God before an unbelieving world; for while he was building the ark of safety, he was able to witness to the scoffers of a destruction coming upon them as a just punishment for their depravity of life and their refusal to accept the one way of salvation God has provided.

   (6) His eternal blessing: he received everlasting life because he was justified by faith; he inherited (not earned) what came to him as a free gift on the basis of a death and the free disposal of the owner's goods to those whom he chooses. Thus Noah presented an example of the operation of justification by faith.

3. (11:8-22) Faith of the pre-Mosaic Patriarchs — faith in its relation to a chosen Family and People of God.

   a. (11:8-19) The Faith of Patient Obedience: Abraham.

      (1) (:8) The faith of self-surrender: having been called by God to leave homeland and kindred (note that the beginning of the Messianic nation was a separating call) he went forth to an unknown land, to receive the inheritance God had promised him. So doing, he gave up all dependence upon visible security and ventured forth in reliance upon the unseen God and His promises. And that

too without any written Scriptures or faithful prophets to look to by way of encouraging example.

(2) **(:9-10)** The faith of patience: even when he was shown by God what land He had promised him, he occupied it only as a sojourner, not enjoying it as his own, but constrained to move about as a nomad, dwelling in tents — he and his son and grandson after him. But there was a hope that buoyed him up and made him content without any certain dwelling-place on earth, for he looked for the heavenly Jerusalem, the City of God — invisible as yet to the human eye, yet more permanent and indestructible than any visible city, because designed and constructed by the Almighty Creator Himself. (This passage discloses that Abraham was well instructed as to the blessed fellowship he would forever enjoy with God in the life to come. Compare with this Christ's amazing statement: "Abraham rejoiced to see My day" — Jn. 8:56).

(3) **(:11)** The faith of influence: Sarah was inspired by her husband's example (although at first she had laughed in unbelief) to believe that once God had promised something, no matter how contrary to nature, He was able to bring it to pass. The practical result: she received ability to conceive a son when she was far too old for that to be a biological possibility (about 88 or 89 years of age).

(4) **(:12)** The glorious reward of self-multiplication and ultimate fulfilment of the promise of Gen. 15:5 and Gen. 22:17: a posterity as numerous as the stars and the sands; — not just a single son but an entire host, a great and numerous nation, all acknowledging him as their forefather (amazingly fulfilled not only in the multiplication of the Hebrew race, but also in the far greater numbers of Gentile Christians, and even in the great honor that hundreds of millions of Moslems have paid him since Mohammed's time).

(5) **(11:13-16)** The essential characteristic of the faith of Abraham and his spiritual descendants: they looked unto, paid heed to, the unseen things

of God's promise and Kingdom, rather than to the transient visible things of this life.

(a) **(:13a)** They died in the faith, still looking forward to the fulfilment of the promise of inheritance — trusting, therefore, in a future life; for though they had not received the fulfilment before death, except by way of a mere token ("having seen them afar off" — e. g. the military triumph over the Four Kings, and the vision of Gen. 15:13-16 which followed after it), yet they gladly welcomed the prospect of the ultimate fulfilment.

(b) **(:13b-14)** They did not regard this earth as their home, but only a place they visited as strangers or resided in as temporary immigrants *(parepidēmoi)*. As Abraham remarked, as he was negotiating with the Hittites for the purchase of the cave of Machpelah, "I am a stranger and sojourner among you." Thus he and his family showed they were really looking for a heavenly fatherland beyond Canaan itself. (So also Christians are to beware of settling down as citizens of this world, but are to keep their gaze directed towards the Heavenly City, to which they properly belong.)

(c) **(:15)** Their following the leading of God to a future, heavenly country in preference to a tangible, earthly possession, was a voluntary choice on their part. They were not compelled; they could have reverted to the status of the rest of mankind and given their soul back to the world so as to become earth-citizens, had they desired to do so. But instead they chose for the Lord's sake to dwell in tents, ready to move on at His bidding, without sinking down their roots anywhere on earth. In their heart they were ever reaching out their hands towards their heavenly homeland which they had never seen. (This insight into the inner attitude of Abraham, Isaac and Jacob is certainly corroborated by the Genesis record; how else can we explain why a former city-dweller avoided ever settling down permanently in any single community and becoming a Canaanite citizen? For one who was raised in a community of such advanced urban culture as Ur, and who spent many years of his early manhood in a trade-center like Haran, Abraham showed a remarkable preference for nomadic life.)

(d) **(:16)** Because they thus founded their whole life upon the reality of the unseen God, and counted on His promises more than upon the material guarantees of this world, they showed themselves to belong in very truth to God's heavenly family. God Himself, therefore, was not ashamed to call Himself their God (e. g. at the burning bush He described Himself as "the God of Abraham, Isaac and Jacob"), but as a faithful parent he has prepared for these His children a city in heaven (Ps. 46:4 "There is a river, the streams whereof shall make glad the *city* of our God, the holy place of the tabernacles of the Most High" — a city which could not refer to Jerusalem, which boasted of no such river).

(6) **(11:17)** Abraham's supreme and decisive act of faith: the sacrifice of Isaac.

(a) Two areas of testing: (i) whether his obedience to God transcended his natural affection for his only-begotten son (the same pathos-laden word as in Jn. 3:16: *monogenēs*), Isaac being the only son he had by Sarah and the only son to receive the spiritual inheritance of the Covenant; (ii) whether he would be willing to obey even when he could not see *why;* when the command of God seemed utterly inconsistent with His previous promise.

(b) Abraham's trust in God was such that he looked for Him to perform His promise despite apparent impossibility. He could not believe that God would go back on His word, even though His new command seemed to make it impossible of fulfilment. Therefore he could only conclude that God intended to raise Isaac from the dead (even though this was at that time an absolutely unprecedented miracle) and had the power to do so.

(c) The deliverance of Isaac nearly amounted to a resurrection from the dead; at least the boy was snatched from the very jaws of death by God's gracious interposition of a sacrificial substitute (the ram provided by Jehovah-jireh, "Jehovah will provide"). Such a last-minute rescue or reprieve was suggestive of the coming resurrection from the dead experienced by the Second Adam, the Son of David and of Abraham.

b. **(11:20-22)** The Faith of Confidence in God's Promise-keeping Faithfulness: Isaac, Jacob and Joseph, who predicted future blessing contrary to natural indications.

(1) *Isaac* blessed Jacob and Esau in such a way as to reverse the natural human order, exalting the younger above the elder (even though his human preference and carnal intention had been to prefer Esau, the elder), bowing to the will of God that Jacob should receive the Covenant inheritance. (As Westcott points out, this incident of the blessing of Jacob and Esau marked a crisis in the fulfilment of God's plan, for here for the first time a choice had to be made between two persons through each of whom the Covenant promise might equally have been fulfilled — twins born of the same wife, rather than a choice between the son of a bondwoman and the son of a free, as had been the case between Ishmael and Isaac.)

(2) *Jacob* blessed each of his twelve sons, venturing to predict confidently what God had disclosed to him in secret. In his case also he preferred the younger, Ephraim, as over against the elder, Manasseh, when laying his hands upon Joseph's two sons.

(3) *Joseph* predicted the Exodus, even though his people were then comfortably settled in Egypt, enjoying high privilege and great influence in the royal court. Nevertheless he looked forward only to the return of his people to the Land of Promise, regarding it as the only proper place for his mortal remains to be ultimately buried.

77

4. **(11:23-31)** The Faith of Moses: preferring Fellowship with God to Enjoyment in the World.

a. **(:23)** In his parents, Moses had a background of confident and daring faith. They were willing to risk punishment or death itself by keeping their baby boy alive; and such was their confidence in God that they committed the infant to a basket in the river, looking for Him somehow to save the helpless child both from death and from the cruelty of a ruthless government. (We have here also the suggestion that there was something in the baby's appearance — he was a "goodly" or well-formed child, as *asteios* implies — which led them to believe that he had a God-appointed destiny.)

b. **(:24-26)** Moses' personal choice for God when still a young man (i. e., about forty years of age): he was willing to give up princely privilege conferred upon him by the world in order to remain perfectly faithful to God, even at the cost of sharing the woes and disrepute of God's afflicted people.

  (1) "The pleasures of sin for a *season*" shows how foolish would be the opposite choice, the brief and transient enjoyment the worldling prefers to getting right with God and living for God. But Moses put God's will first, and thus guaranteed to himself eternal blessing.

  (2) Because this man of faith saw that God's will and glory comes first, he esteemed it precious and worthwhile to share in the reproach leveled at Christ by the world, rather than to enjoy the curse-laden luxury and wealth of this world.

  (3) "The reproach of Christ" — what did Moses have to do with Christ? This significant phase shows us that the pre-incarnate Christ was present among God's people and suffered with God's people (cf. Ps. 89:50-51) even back in the days of the Exodus (when His presence was symbolized by the Pillar of cloud and of fire). It also shows that all of the people of God, even prior to the birth of Jesus, were united with Him in interest and already belonged to Him as His precious possession (Ex. 19:5), because of the price which He had agreed with the Father that He would pay on Calvary (Eph. 1:4-5; 2 Tim. 1:9).

78

(4) **(:26c)** Moses valued things according to their ultimate goal and destination, rather than according to the immediate advantage they seemed to hold out to him.

c. **(11:27)** Moses' self-committal to God's invisible providence when he became a leader responsible for his own people.

   (1) God's promise of deliverance was still unsupported by any external proof, and had to be accepted by sheer faith in the face of insuperable odds, as it seemed; but Pharoah's power to hurt and destroy was most tangible and evident to the eye. Yet Moses was willing to believe God's naked promise and trust that he and his people could leave Egypt without scathe from a heavily armed and brutal oppressor.

   (2) Thus Moses showed that the God whom he could not see with the physical eye was more real to him than those mortal persons whom he could see. Therefore as in God's presence Moses "endured," i. e. he persevered *(ekarterēsen)*, valiantly persisting in his chosen course.

   (3) **(11:28)** Moses showed faith also in celebrating the Passover in Egypt, relying on God's unproved assurance that He would do something which had never happened before: (a) that the first-born and only the first-born of all the Egyptians would die of plague on a single night; (b) that the mere sprinkling of lamb's blood on the doorposts would save the Israelite first-born from this plague. (This was an unprecedented, unique event. Note how characteristically God has carried out His program of redemption through unique acts: the Flood, the Virgin Birth, the bodily Resurrection. Because unique, these events lie utterly outside the field of science, for science can investigate only that which repeatedly or customarily happens. Therefore science can say nothing relevant to these great redemptive acts recorded in Scripture.)

d. **(11:29-30)** The faith of the Israelites under Moses: the faith which goes forward in the face of physical "impossibilities."

(1) The death-dealing barrier of the Red Sea was transformed into a highway of safety when God's people responded to Him in faith. But as soon as the God-defying Egyptians attempted the same line of travel, it became to them a snare of destruction. (This exposes the folly of attempting the way of "faith" while by-passing the Cross and the authority of God's word.)

(2) Again at Jericho the next generation under Joshua was willing to obey God and trust His promise, even in the face of the ridicule of the jeering worldlings who thronged the walls of that powerful city to watch them go through an apparently absurd piece of mummery simply because God had told them to do so. The result: God threw down the walls with a mighty earthquake. In this overthrow of Jericho God provided His people with a physical illustration of a spiritual law: that nothing can withstand those who are wholly committed to the Lord. (So also the physical healings performed by Christ and the Apostles: they symbolized His power to heal the sin-sick soul. So also the sudden death of Ananias and Sapphira in Acts 5: this exemplary punishment of professing Christians was intended to warn the Church for all time to come, that God accepts as His redeemed only those who are sincere in their faith and do not attempt to lie to Him. Since the spiritual law was thus adequately symbolized by the physical event, it was not necessary for the physical symbol ever to be repeated after the first period of education was over.)

e. **(11:31)** The faith of Gentile converts who joined themselves to the people of Moses.

(1) Destruction impended the accursed Gentile city of Jericho, depraved and altogether ripe for judgment; but the harlot, Rahab, who had been as guilty as the rest of her people, was nevertheless saved from the common destruction because she submitted to the One True God.

(2) She evidenced her new faith by confessing it, first of all, to the Hebrew spies (Jos. 2:11), and then by risking her own life by enabling them to escape.

80

5. **(11:32-38)** Faith as shown by the heroic leaders and prophets of Israel subsequent to the Exodus.
   a. The glorious victories of those who trusted God (11:32-35a).
      (1) Heroes from the time of the Judges: Gideon (Jg. 6-8), Barak (Jg. 4-5), Samson (Jg. 16) and Jephtha (Jg. 11-12). Each overcame a different God-defying foe: (i) the Midianites (ii) the North Canaanites (iii) the Philistines (iv) the Ammonites.
      (2) Those representing the Monarchy: David (who was a prophet as well as a king, cf. Ac. 2:30), Samuel (the prophet who was the anointer of kings), and the other prophets. (Thus in these judges, kings and prophets we have adequately represented the chief classes of notable believers under the Theocracy and the Monarchy.)
      (3) **(11:33-35a)** The characteristic achievements of God-trusting faith.
         (a) The general types of success they achieved: (a) they defeated kingdoms, that is, invaders who opposed them with numerically superior forces (e. g. Gideon's three hundred against the myriads of Midian); (b) they brought righteousness to pass, i. e. they enforced justice (as was testified of David in II Sa. 8:15, and of Samuel in I Sa. 12:4); (c) they "obtained" or attained to *(epetykhon)* God's promises, i. e. the fulfilment of promises already made (as Isaiah lived to see Jerusalem delivered from Sennacherib, and Daniel the release of the exiled Jews from Babylon).
         (b) Their personal deliverances: (a) from lions, the most fearsome of beasts (Samson, David, Daniel) (b) from fire, the most painful of physical forces (Shadrach, Meshach and Abednego) (c) from the sword of ungodly tyranny (David from Saul, Elijah from Ahab and Ahaziah, Elisha from Jehoram and Benhadad).
         (c) The attainment of personal gifts for God's service: (a) strength out of weakness (Samson, David, Hezekiah after illness) (b) the exhibi-

tion of strength in warfare (Gideon against the Midianites, Jonathan against the Philistines at Michmash) (c) routing the enemy in battle (perhaps the words "armies of the aliens" — *parembolas allotriōn* — are meant to suggest the remarkable victories of the valiant Maccabees, since both of these words are characteristic of *I Maccabees* in the Apocrypha).

(d) Climactic instance, the most notable achievement of faith in the physical realm: restoring the dead to life once more (as Elijah did to the widow's son at Zarephath, I Ki. 17:17, and Elisha to the Shunamite's son in II Ki. 4:17).

b. The victorious sufferings of those who trusted God (11:35b-38).

(1) **(35b-36)** Constancy in the face of proffered release for surrendering convictions.

(a) Sufferings unto death (:35b).

(i) Some were "tortured" (*tympanizō* implies that they were stretched upon a rack as hide is stretched over a drum, *tympanon*, and then beaten to death), even though their tormentors offered them their life if they would forswear their loyalty to God.

(ii) The faith which buoyed up through martyrdom: they looked for a resurrection far better than mere survival for a few more years in this present evil world (cf. II Macc. 7:9, where a Jewish martyr says: "Thou, miscreant, dost release us out of this present life, but the King of the world shall raise us up who have died for His laws, unto an eternal renewal of life").

(b) Sufferings not unto death (:36):
They were tested by "mockings" (*empaigmoi* — a term including cruel, sportive forms of treatment of all kinds) and by scourging with whips (thus Jeremiah, when he was put into the stocks by Pashhur, Je. 20), by bonds and

imprisonment (Micaiah by Ahab, Jeremiah by Irijah).

(2) **(:37-38)** More general forms of suffering under persecution.

    (a) Sufferings unto death (:37a) : (i) death by stoning (Zechariah, son of Jehoiada, 2 Chr. 24:20-22; Naboth by the agents of Jezebel, I Ki. 21:13) (ii) death by being sawed in two (a fate which tradition assigns to Isaiah in the days of Manasseh) (iii) death (or murder — *phonos*) by the tyrant's sword (the hundreds of prophets slain at the order of Jezebel, I Ki. 19:10; Urijah slain by Jehoiakim, Jer. 26:23).

    (b) Sufferings not unto death (:37b-38) : (a) poverty and homelessness (Elijah, who went in a goatskin or sheepskin, I Ki. 19:13, without any settled home as he fled from Ahab's police) ; (b) lack of the barest necessities of life (*hysteroumenoi* — "destitute") (c) enduring hardship and affliction generally, as they felt the malice of the ungodly world; (d) ostracism and exile, expelled from the comforts of civilization and social intercourse to lead a fugitive existence in the deserts, mountains and caves, even though they were spiritually more deserving than all the ungodly world which persecuted them (such were David and Elijah). (Note that these noble believers were all victims of flagrant injustice. Yet this unmerited suffering is recounted to their glory; from heaven's viewpoint, it was an honor for them thus to be unfairly treated for the Lord's sake. How blind of us not to see this and to begin to murmur against God when we find ourselves unfairly treated!)

(3) **(11:39-40)** The general characteristic of these O. T. heroes of faith: their disregard of earthly values and their forward look to the eventual fulfilment of God's promises.

    (a) These all died without having personally experienced the fulfilment of the blessing on earth which God had promised would come. Yet their patient endurance in the absence of such material proof, their willingness to account God's promise as sure and certain as if already fulfilled, this is what demonstrated a faith which God could approve as such, and which He could attest as marking them as Covenant children of His own holy family (the "having obtained a good report" is more literally "having been attested to" *martyrē-thentes* sc. by God Himself).

(b) **(11:40)** God's purpose in deferring the reward for their faith (that is, the reward of the Messiah and His Kingdom) was that as many as possible of future generations might be included in the embrace of God's love in His family of the redeemed.

(i) God's better plan was the New Testament economy, according to which the doors of salvation were thrown wide open to all nations, and that too on the basis of an already accomplished work of redemption, not simply on the basis of a redemption yet to come.

(ii) Without use of the N. T. dispensation these O. T. stalwarts of the faith were not "made perfect." What is meant by this making perfect *(teleioō)*? Probably the completion of the whole process of redemption. This cannot mean simply the payment of the ransom price on Calvary, for even the N. T. Apostles like Paul are still looking forward to a consummation to be attained only when the Resurrection of the bodies of believers takes place and Christ returns to earth to establish His Millennial Kingdom (cf. Rom. 8:23). Hence it follows that even we of the N. T. age will not be made perfect either, until the last generation of Christians has been added to the Body of Christ prior to His return.

C. The Surpassing Power of New Testament Faith, on the Basis of the Victory Christ has already Won (Chap. 12).

l. **(12:1-11)** Victory through the encouragement of Christ's example and the discipline of sonship.

  a. **(12:1)** Encouragement from these heroes who have proved the overcoming power of faith.

    (1) The inspiration of these spiritual forebears of ours: (a) they are living demonstrations of the power of God available to those who believe Him and are wholly committed to Him. From the pages of Scripture they testify to us of God's power to show forth his glory and deliverance in response to faith. (b) They surround us like a cloud of witnesses in an amphitheater (*perikeimenon* — "surrounding" makes the idea of a circle of spectators quite explicit) watching us from above like hovering clouds in the sky, and encouraging us in the footrace in which we of the present generation are engaged. (Delitzsch: "Once witnesses for God, they are now witnesses of us their brethren: the two notions are closely intertwined. Our life here is a contest, its theater the universe, the seats of the spectators are ranged through heaven.")

    (2) Consequent stimulus to the Christian, who stands in their succession, to make the running of the race the supreme motive in this life, and stripping off every hindrance and sin for maximum efficiency. When we regard the blessed end-achievement of these heroic predecessors of ours, it becomes very easy for us to forsake and forswear any rival claim to our loyalty and interest but that of Christ Himself.

     (a) **(12:1b)** One type of hindrance is the "weight," the superfluous burden (like obesity in a trackman) which is composed of slowness and dullness of spiritual perceptions, or of the encumbrance of Judaic rites and observances which have now become obsolete.

     (b) A second type is described as "easily besetting" (*euperistatos* — readily encircling for ambush and entrapment) sin, that is the sin which comes in a concealed or disguised form, pretending to be innocuous, but fiercely pouncing upon its victim in his moments of relaxed vigilance.

(c) Note that the Christian's life is here viewed as an athletic contest *(agōn)*, like a race at the Olympic Games, with a specific goal or prize in view. It is not a leisurely pleasure-saunter, as the flesh would prefer to have it.

(d) It is not to be run by straining and tense effort, but by patient endurance *(hypomonē* — "a steadfast remaining under the load")* in carrying on the race.

b. **(12:2-3)** Powerful encouragement from Christ's example unto cheerful endurance.

(1) The attitude needful for the Christian runner: "looking unto," that is, looking away *(aphorōntes)* from all lesser values and unworthy distractions, so as to center one's gaze upon Jesus Himself (the opposite of looking at other Christians for the purpose of censorious criticism, or of finding flimsy justification for personal compromise with sin).

(2) The twofold influence of Christ: (a) as the perfect Man and suffering Servant He stands before us as the most perfect exemplar of faith, as our Captain or Leader (rather than "author," which is inaccurate for *arkhēgos*) of the martyr-army of O. T. heroes, but surpassing them all in the purity and fulness of His faith; (b) as the "Finisher" or Perfecter *(teleiōtēs)* of our faith, the One who has by His sufferings and entrance into Glory completed the work of our redemption. Having attained the goal or prize Himself, He leads all who follow Him to persevere unto the same mark.

(3) Reminder of how He won this prize: by enduring crucifixion, the supreme humiliation for the Lord of heaven and earth; and not merely enduring it, but esteeming the suffering but a very little thing in comparison with the glorious prize He attained by means of it: the redemption of God's elect people from the guilt of sin and power of hell, the exalting of the Father in victorious love by the defeat of the malignant hatred of Satan, His foe.

(4) The reward which Christ has won: the Lordship (as the God-Man, the Second Adam, the sinners' High Priest) over all God's universe, ruling as

viceroy for the Trinity. Having endured the cross, He now wears the crown.

(5) **(12:3)** The Christian runner is bidden to make a careful estimate or reckoning (*analogizomai* — "consider") of this example of Christ's in relation to his own problems of suffering.

    (a) Christ had to put up with contradiction or contrary argument *(antilogia)*, even though He Himself was always perfectly in the right, and that too from wretched sinners. (Such unwarranted and unjustified hostility far exceeded any unfairness or ingratitude Christians shall ever be called upon personally to endure.)

    (b) Then it will be apparent that your personal trials are not nearly so severe as His were. If, then, He endured far sorer trial than you, there is no reason why you should not cheerfully endure the far lesser testings that come your way. There is no excuse for becoming enfeebled and exhausted in your soul, whether because of self-pity or because of bitter criticism of God's dealings. (If God allowed far worse to befall His only Son, what right has a Christian to complain at the undeserved suffering which may come into his life?)

c. **(12:4-11)** Chastenment of Christians is ordained by Parental Love and results in deepened spirituality.

(1) **(:4)** Christians should be prepared to lay down their very life for the sake of the Gospel; why should they be discouraged, then, at any persecution short of death?

    (a) "Not yet" implies that they may some day be subjected to martyrdom, even though they have been spared that so far; "unto blood" suggests the supreme sacrifice which Jesus Himself offered up for our redemption.

    (b) "Resisted . . . striving against sin" — this implies that the Christian's life must be a continual warfare without compromise, not a comfortable settling down, accepting conditions as they are in this sin-dominated world, nor yet accepting as unconquerable and unchangeable the imperfections and inconsistencies of their own carnal nature.

(2) **(12:5-6)** Undeserved hardship is explicitly included in God's promises for Christians; it is a necessary part of his pathway to heaven's glory (into which the Father "receives" His children when they attain to the final Canaan-rest) .

  (a) "Ye have forgotten"; your spiritual problem (i. e. your discouragement and tendency to yield before the pressures of the world) results from forgetting something which you have been carefully warned of by the Scriptures.

  (b) Proof text: Prov. 3:11-12: "The chastening of Jehovah, my son, do not despise, and do not abhor His rebuke; for whom Jehovah loves He rebukes even as a father the son whom he favorably receives (or: is pleased with) ." This implies: (i) there is a real danger that a believer may receive chastenment in the wrong way, and that such a response on his part implies a contempt or abhorrence for something which God has in His wisdom permitted him to undergo; bitterness or complaint under these circumstances becomes an almost blasphemous offense against the Almighty Himself; (ii) the animating motive in sending this discipline is God's fatherly love.

(3) **(12:7-10)** Why hardship and suffering are a necessary and justified part of God's education of His children for heaven.

  (a) **(:7a)** The purpose of the hardship Christians have to endure (*hypomenō* — cf. *hypomonē* in 12:1) is *paideia,* a term which embraces the chastening of children *(paides),* their discipline or training generally, and then (as it pertains to their intellect and spiritual nature) their education.

  (b) **(:7b)** This chastening is to be received with gratitude as a seal of our status as true sons of God, since God is hereby dealing with us as a true Father.

88

(c) **(:8)** Conversely, if Christians were to escape any *paideia*, this might indicate, not fatherly favor, but the neglect and indifference a man might show towards a spurious child (*nothos* — "bastard"; presumably a product of marital infidelity, hence a hypocritical professor who tries to serve both God and Mammon at the same time), who is not regarded as truly belonging to God's household.

(d) **(:9a)** Proof of this view is found in the policy of human fathers, who despite their human defects at least show forth this principle as inherent in fatherhood.

(e) **(:9b)** *A fortiori,* since we human children reverence and respect our fathers for exercising this prerogative and duty of chastement, we must all the more show a filial reverence and submission of will toward our Heavenly Father when He disciplines us, rather than descending into bitterness, complaint, rebelliousness or discouragement (the reactions of the fallen man, dead in trespasses and sins). Such a godly and filial response on our part is evidence of a true state of salvation and of the indwelling life *(zōē)* of Christ, in Whom and by Whom we shall live *(zaō)*.

(f) **(:10)** *A fortiori* also, if we appreciate as necessary and proper the discipline of children by earthly and fallible human parents, how much more should we accept with appreciation the rigorous training of the infallible God, who always contrives for our ultimate advantage — especially when that advantage or benefit is the greatest of all possible blessings: the partaking of God's holy nature and character in a fuller measure than ever before?

(4) **(12:11)** The unpleasantness of the chastening hardship should not cause us any discouragement, for hardship is not supposed to be anything but unpleasant; in its very nature it is grievous, and the fact that it proves to be so is no ground whatever for disillusionment or bitterness, or for doubting that the result will be beneficial. The benefit

89

("fruit") in this case is peace, an inner peace of heart in which the believer abides (Hab. 3:18 "Yet will I rejoice in Jehovah," despite the loss of all earthly possessions and security, "I will joy in the God of my salvation"), a peace which can only result from a conscience free from the rebuke of any known sin unconfessed and unjudged — "the peaceable fruit of *righteousness.*" Note also that the disciplining hardship is here referred to as a gymnastic training ("exercised" is *gegymnasmenois* from *gymnazō*) appropriate for an athlete preparing for victory.

2. **(12:12-17)** Encouragement to harmony, holiness and care of the brethren.

a. **(:12-14)** Learning from the discipline of suffering, we are to strive for peace with others and devotion towards God.

(1) **(:12-13)** Appreciating the beneficial results of discipline, the believer will lay aside all feelings of discouragement.

(a) Such a spirit of good cheer and high courage is enjoined in Is. 35:3 (the "Highway of Holiness" chapter) as being a characteristic of those who are truly on God's highway to glory": "Strengthen the hands which hang limp and fortify the stumbling knees."

(b) The attitude of careful attention to the foremost issues of life is commended in Pr. 4:26 "Make smooth the path of thy foot, and let all of thy ways be firmly established," after a warning against a perverted mouth and an admonition to keep the eyes ever looking forward towards the ultimate goal of life. Thus we make our own pathway well-balanced and smooth by remembering to put first the will of God (the theme of Prov. chap. 4) and to leave aside all bitter complaint or preoccupation with the mere temporary concerns of this life (such as recovery from illness or financial poverty, or the like).

(c) A limb which is lame may be utterly thrown out of joint if it is not properly bound up and cared for; even so the natural weakness and

90

imperfection of the carnal nature may become infected with rebellious bitterness, unless we hold to this insight concerning the benevolent Purpose behind affliction. But if we keep intent upon the goal of the Christian race, we shall yield our heart to the Lord even in the midst of trial, and thus the lameness of a soul tempted to bitterness will be healed.

(2) **(12:14)** The pursuit of harmony and holiness.

    (a) This conquest over discouragement paves the way for eager pursuit of peace (harmony) with all other men (especially, all other Christians). Note that disharmony results from self-pity and discontent, which are often vented upon others, who are belittled for the sake of compensatory self-exaltation.

    (b) Peace with fellow-Christians is a prerequisite for a true walk of holiness. Note that holiness is implanted in every born-again believer at the moment of conversion, but the implanted seed will develop as it should only when the principle, "Not I but Christ," gains increasing control over the entire personality (like the gradual warming of a pan set over an electric plate). This process of bringing out Christ's likeness within the soul constitutes an indispensable preparation for heaven. If the process does not go on at all, this is proof positive that the professing believer has never been born again and remains an unsaved sinner. He shall not "see God."

b. **(12:15-17)** Care for fellow-Christians, that they may avoid quarreling, unchastity, or trifling away their Inheritance.

    (1) **(:15a)** A sanctified Christian is to exercise the solicitude of a pastor who watches over (*episkopeō* — to oversee, not simply to "look diligently") his flock, rather than the carnal attitude which all too often characterizes relations between church-members, that of competition for personal influence or recognition, masked beneath a polite and pious exterior. To each church member the others in the congregation are his parish, to protect and heal

and to restore if backslidden, rather than to criticize and condemn and abandon when they seem to fall into error.

(2) The dangers against which each Christian, as a sanctified steward and servant of his brethren, is to be on guard:

   (a) **(:15b)** lest they fail to lay hold by a true and intelligent faith upon the grace of God for salvation and victory:

   (b) lest hard feelings arise between church-members to embitter their souls, embroiling them in an attitude of antagonism and infecting them with the pernicious virus of lovelessness, so that they take their stand with Satan in accusing the saints (Zec. 3:1).

   (c) Note that the phrase "root of bitterness" comes from De. 29:17, where Moses admonishes Israel to remember how abominable were the idols of Egypt, lest there be a person or family or tribe in Israel which turns away its heart from Jehovah to go and serve the gods of these Gentiles, "lest there be in you a root which produces gall and wormwood" — an expression quoted also by Peter in his stern warning to Simon the Magician in Ac. 8:23. In both cases the bitterness is connected with fatal backsliding and apostasy.

   (d) **(:16)** An example of the fatal neglect of the grace of God and of being defiled by the up-springing of a root of bitterness: the example of Esau, who for the sake of a trifling and transient satisfaction (a savory meal) bartered away his birthright, that is, his status as the first-born son, who receives a double portion of his father's inheritance.

     (i) Note that Esau is here spoken of as a "fornicator," presumably in allusion to his marrying out of the faith — for he took a Hittite idolatress to wife — and the assuming of the viewpoints and standards of the pagan Canaanites around him. Also he was a "profane" man; not that he used profanity, necessarily, but he withheld his heart from sanctification (*bebēlos* is the opposite of *hagios*, "holy," and implies a character which recognizes only earthly, materialistic values) ; never did he separate himself from the world and the self-life and set himself apart for God.

(ii) **(12:17)** This profaning of the holy trust committed to him by God brought to Esau eternal loss, which no amount of carnal regret or tearful supplication could win back (because of course his regret arose from contemplating the baneful results of sin rather than because of the sin itself). Note how dishonorable was his request to his father, for he had made a bargain with Jacob to sell him his birthright, and yet now he wished to go back on it simply because Isaac was partial to him. This regret, then, did not amount to a genuine change of heart, and therefore fell short of a true repentance which would have qualified him to be restored by God's grace.

3. **(12:18-29)** The N. T. sanctions for holy living are even more binding than those of the O. T.

a. **(:18-21)** The fearfulness of the O. T. approach to God as symbolized by Mt. Sinai.

(1) **(12:18-19)** The O. T. revelation of God's holiness was through a material, sense-perceptible symbol ("that might be touched") , and that too a symbol accompanied by terrifying manifestations of destructive power: volcanic fire, blackness, gloom and whirlwind, threatening judgment upon the sinful world (Ex. 20:18-20) . (Query: why did a loving and gracious God thus terrify His people at Mt. Sinai? Because the most loving and gracious thing He could do for them at that stage of their education was to convince them that He and He alone was sovereign over all creation, that every soul was answerable to Him, and that they were sinners in need of a Savior. In a believer's experience even today, Sinai must precede Calvary.) There was also

the blast of a mighty trumpet, suggestive of the Last Judgment, and the proclamation of God's holy law in the Ten Commandments, before which the congregation of Israel felt utterly condemned and in need of mercy.

(2) **(:20)** This revelation was of such an awesome character that Israel could not endure to receive any more of it directly from God, being conscious (a) of their worthiness to die, having by sin forfeited the right to live before God (b) aware of God's ability to snuff them out at any moment.

(3) **(:21)** Not only the people themselves but also the human mediator and lawgiver, Moses himself, felt such a fear in the presence of God as He displayed His holy wrath upon sin, that he had to tremble before Him. In Deut. 9:19 Moses later recalled to his people how during his second forty-day fast on the mountain, occasioned by Israel's sin in worshiping the golden calf, "For I was afraid in the presence of the anger and indignation with which Jehovah was wroth against you."

b. **(12:22-24)** The even greater solemnity of the N. T. access to God in His heavenly presence.

(1) **(12:22-23a)** The Christian revelation seen in its fulfilment.

(a) The scene of Mt. Zion:

(i) Its foundation: heavenly archetype of Zion (which doubtless includes Mt. Moriah, on which the Temple was built, where God dwelt in the midst of His people and met them in grace, making it the focal point of His sovereign power, according to Ps. 2:6 and 110:2, etc.) representing the strong foundation of the New Order.

(ii) Its structure: the City of the Living God, the social structure in which the New Order is embodied — such is the Heavenly Jerusalem, the City "which hath foundations" for which Abraham looked (11:10). This is the City, made up of all the redeemed, whose name will be inscribed upon all true believers (Rev.

94

3:12), and which will appear as Christ's Bride upon His return to earth (Rev. 21:2), descending from heaven to earth, containing the radiant glory of God and surrounded by the symbolic twelve-gated wall of Rev. 21:11-12.

- (b) The persons in Zion:
  - (i) **(:22c)** Angels, who are now closely associated with human believers, no longer separated from them as they were at Mt. Sinai, assembled together in their countless myriads as in festal assembly *(panēgyris)* to welcome and fellowship with redeemed mankind.
  - (ii) Men: that is the congregation *(ekklēsia* or "church," representing the O. T. *qāhāl* or "congregation")* of the ransomed believers who are by faith united to Christ, the Firstborn *(prōtotokos* Heb. 1:6) and are therefore counted as "firstborn" *(prōtotokoi)* in Him. (Or else possibly this term "firstborn" may refer to the great pioneers of faith mentioned in Chap. 11, with whom even the humblest believer enjoys the fullest fellowship in heaven.

- (2) **(12:23b-24)** The Christian revelation seen in its efficacy.
  - (a) The Judgment, after earthly life is over.
    - (i) The Judge: the God of all the universe, whose judgment is more than the imposition of penalties; it is the manifestation of right, the vindication of truth.
    - (ii) Those vindicated at this Judgment: those who have died in the faith, who are here described as (1) "spirits" not yet clothed upon with a resurrection-body, but enjoying conscious fellowship with God (cf. Rev. 6:9, where "souls" is similarly used — such passages as these leave no room for the error of "soul sleep") (2) "just" or "righteous" because justified by Grace through faith in Christ, and indwelt by

His Holy Spirit (3) "having been made perfect," that is, made perfect in holiness, having attained the end or goal for which they were created and redeemed (the passive participle *teteleiōmenōn* indicating that this perfecting was done to them by Christ in response to their faith, rather than by personal effort on their own part).

(b) The gift of Grace: life continued on in heaven, on a glorified plane.

    (i) The most glorious gift of all: the Lord Jesus Himself, who is the inheritance and portion of every citizen of Heavenly Zion under the New Covenant.

    (ii) The New Covenant itself (here described as *nea*, "new" in the sense of "recent" or "fresh"; instead of *kainē* "of a different kind," as it was designated in 8:8 and elsewhere) mediated to the N. T. people of God through a Messianic Moses, and therefore conferring both a superior blessing and a heavier responsibility.

    (iii) The Atonement or "blood of sprinkling:" i. e. the typical sprinkling with blood which Moses employed in validating the Old Covenant with Israel as a nation has now been fulfilled by the shedding of Christ's atoning blood. The blood of Abel (and, by implication, of the other O. T. martyrs) witnessed to the world of unbelievers concerning their guilt and folly, and called for their just punishment by the Divine Judge. But the blood of Jesus speaks to the believer something far better: the self-sacrificing love of that Judge who has paid the death-penalty Himself in the sinner's place.

c. **(12:25)** *A fortiori,* even greater condemnation results from disregarding the Gospel than the Law (i. e. the O. T. Torah).

(1) There is a terrible penalty awaiting those who have heard the voice of Christ speaking to them

96

from heaven (as He does speak through His written Word, His living messengers and His Holy Spirit) and who nevertheless reject or "refuse" Him (i. e. *paraiteomai* — "ask to have oneself excused from" an invitation or responsibility, the same word as in Lu. 14:18, the Parable of the Great Supper).

(2) This condemnation of the rejecters of God's call was severe enough in the case of Moses' generation, who in their rebellions and "murmurings" turned away from God's guidance and revealed will. They certainly did not escape judgment, for they all ultimately died in the wilderness without ever seeing the Promised Land. (Note that the best Greek manuscripts place the "upon earth" between "escaped not" and "refused" rather than after "spake." The translation should read: "For those men did not escape on earth after they had sought to excuse themselves from Him who divinely spoke to them." Even though they were only creatures of clay dwelling on earth, they presumptuously rebelled against Jehovah and turned their back upon their Covenant undertakings towards Him.)

(3) Therefore there must be for us of this new era a far graver penalty if we turn away from God the Son, whose voice comes to us from the Holy of Holies in heaven, where Christ sits enthroned in power, communicating His will through His Apostles under the inspiration of the Holy Spirit.

d. **(12:26-29)** Consequent need of reverently holding to Divine Grace, forsaking the temporal things of earth for the eternal Kingdom of Heaven.

(1) **(:26-27)** All the more solemn is our duty not to turn away from Christ's heavenly call, because His voice is also the voice of judgment upon the whole material world.

    (a) In token of judgment to come, God's voice thundering down from Sinai shook the whole mountain, as God manifested Himself to Moses and the Israelites in Ex. 19:18 ". . . and all the mountain shook exceedingly."

    (b) Hag. 2:6 shows that this shaking of Sinai had a prophetic significance, pointing to the End

Time: "Yet once, it is a little while, and I will shake the heavens, the earth, the sea and the dry land." In other words, God will shake the earth again as He did in the day when He gave the Ten Commandments.

(c) Note that this shaking of the land and sea is spoken of in such a way by Haggai as to imply more than a mere earthquake. Hence all material creation is to be shaken, and therefore also done away with, to make way for the unveiling of the eternal and unshakable realities of God's Kingdom in glory. (Doubtless these realities include the heavenly archetypes of the earthly symbols of Tabernacle and Temple.)

(2) **(:28)** The only proper response for a believer who is relying on these unshakable realities of heaven: a constant gratitude towards God.

(a) Note that the unshakable kingdom of God is something to be received from God's outstretched hand; it is not something which men bring in by their collective effort or wisely conceived programs for social reform or for economic and political improvement.

(b) It is by a life expressing gratitude that we can please God with our worship and service. (Here note that the older rendering, "Let us have grace" fails to take stock of the fact that wherever else in the N. T. *kharin ekhein* occurs, Lk. 17:9; I Ti. 1:12; II Ti. 1:3, it signifies "to be thankful to someone." It so happens that the word for "grace" and for "gratitude" are the same, but with *ekhein* "to have" it practically always means "gratitude.")

(c) But this attitude of unceasing gratefulness is to be accompanied by godly reverence and a fear or abhorrence of disobeying the will of God.

(d) **(12:29)** Such a fear is all the more befitting since our N. T. God is the same as the O. T. God who revealed Himself at Sinai as a burning fire. (In this connection Herveius points that fire has four functions: (i) to burn up

98

the trash of sin; (ii) to dry out the humor or moisture of lust residing in the heart; (iii) to illumine the mind with a knowledge of the truth; (iv) to set the soul aflame with Christ's love. In this passage, however, it is plainly the fire of judgment and of refining away dross and slag which the author has in view.)

This verse is quoted from Deut. 4:24: "For Jehovah thy God, He is a devouring fire, a jealous God." This statement was made by Moses after he had warned Israel not to forget the Covenant and fall into idolatry after they cross the Jordan River. Compare the assertion of John the Baptist concerning Christ: "But He will burn up the chaff with unquenchable fire" (Mat. 3:12) — a prediction doubtless referring to His Second Coming. Yet notice the verse just preceding (Mat. 3:11) : "He shall baptize you with the Holy Ghost and with fire."

D. The Surpassing Godliness Made Available by the Surpassing Power (Chap. 13).

1. **(13:1-6)** Liberation from selfish niggardliness, self-centeredness, impurity and covetousness (the Social Duties).

   a. **(:1-3)** Sympathy.

      (1) **(:1)** Brotherly love lies at the foundation of all the Christian's ethical relationships, as a member by adoption of God's holy family, a family to which all who are born again belong. It is not enough to feel this loving sentiment towards other Christians at the start of the Christian life, in the first glow of conversion, but it is to continue on even when personalities clash and differences of viewpoint arise. Only then is the real quality of Christian love brought to the fore, and differentiated from the cordiality of the natural man towards those who agree with him and avoid crossing his will.

      (2) **(:2)** A practical evidence of this brother-love is hospitality, an inclusion of others in the provision God has made for His family, who are to share His material benefits as need and occasion arise.

(a) This hospitality is to be extended even towards strangers (since the word for "hospitality," *(philoxenia)* is compounded with the word *xenos,* "stranger"), as is beautifully exampled to us by Abraham, who unexpectedly found himself host to angels (Gen. 18) when he followed his usual custom of kindness to passing wayfarers.

(3) **(:3)** A second practical outworking of brotherly love is visitation of those in prison, especially of imprisoned Christians.

(a) This visitation is not to be done as a mere discharge of duty but in a spirit of heartfelt sympathy as if actually suffering the same imprisonment and hardship (even as God suffers with His children in their affliction — Is. 63:9).

(b) A further factor in sympathetic compassion: the Christian sympathizer is himself still in his pre-Resurrection body and therefore capable of enduring similar sufferings at the hands of unjust men some time in the future.

b. **(13:4)** Faithfulness in marriage (the closest of all social ties and the most binding of duties).

(1) In the case of all Christians (no room here for a celibate clergy!) marriage is not only permitted but also honorable. (Note that the verb "is" does not appear in the Greek, although it is fairly assumed. There is, however, some ground for supplying, "Let there be" *estō* — instead of "is" — *esti.* In that case it would mean: "Let marriage be held in honor among all, and let the bed be undefiled." This rendering is favored by the construction used in the following verse, in which again the verb "to be" is omitted, but is quite certainly to be supplied as *estō,* "Let . . . be . . .")

(2) Violation of the marriage vow (standing as it does for a sacred symbol of Christ united with His Church and completely faithful to it) is a crime against God. Even though it may go unpunished by men, God will certainly execute judgment upon those who defile the marriage bed by adultery.

c. **(13:5-6)** Freedom from the money motive.

(1) The character of a Christian who has entered the Promised Land by faith must be free from covetousness (*aphilargyros* — "not-money-loving") , that is, a love of money for its own sake and for personal advantage in this life.

(2) The true believer regards whatever God sends him in answer to prayer as quite sufficient for his needs, and therefore he is cheerfully content with whatever he has, so far as material necessities are concerned.

(3) Failure to be content and to trust in God's material provision amounts to a denial of what the Scripture says about God's faithfulness — hence is tantamount to blasphemy.

(4) The Scripture says (in Josh. 1:5, where Joshua is about to invade Canaan) : "I will not leave thee nor forsake thee." (This follows after the assurance that as God had been with Moses, so He would be with Joshua himself.)

(5) Therefore this freedom from the money motive even in the routine of daily bread-winning really follows from the central testimony of a Christian's whole life: that God is his Redeemer.

   (a) **(13:6)** So also in Ps. 118:6: "Jehovah is mine; I will not fear what man will do to me." Note that this Psalm (118) , often sung at religious festivals, was quoted several times elsewhere in the N. T. (v. 22 "the stone which the builders rejected" in Lk. 20:17 and elsewhere, and "Hosannah! Blessed is He that cometh in the name of the Lord" — v. 26 — in Mk. 11:9) . It is one of the most joyous expressions of thanksgiving to be found in the O. T., extolling the lovingkindness of God and His gracious deliverance of Israel from all their distress.

2. **(13:7)** Respect for and imitation of the leaders of the Church.

   a. Remember those who used to lead you (the first apostles and evangelists, the pastors and teachers) , that their godly influence may be evident in your life.

   b. In two respects they are to be remembered and their example followed: (i) the sound Gospel, the message revealed by God and not invented by man, which they

faithfully preached to you in soul-searching and up-
lifting sermons; (ii) their godly life, which they led as
those who were dead to self and alive unto God, suffering with Christ and for Christ, and wherever necessary, laying down their physical lives in martyrdom;
(iii) "the end of their conversation," i. e. the manner
of their exit *(ekbasis)* from this life, thus bringing to a
close their earthly *anastrophē* ("conversation" or "conduct of life") the way in which they behaved before
men in every time of testing, and in the attitude of
love which they displayed before all observers.

   c. Remembering their example they are to imitate their
faith (i. e. their trust in Christ and their faithfulness
to Christ), that guiding principle and driving force
which made them mighty and fruitful for God.

3. **(13:8-9)** The Unchanging Christ guarantees the steadfastness of those who hold firmly to Christian Doctrine.

   a. **(:8)** The substance of the faith of these deceased
Christian leaders: the unchangeableness of Christ Himself.

      (1) Because He is the same, therefore His plan and
program will always be the same. Therefore a
Christian may give his life to carrying out the
redemptive plan of conquest, confident that his
labors are worth while no matter what the cost,
and that his life will count for the "Kingdom
which cannot be moved" (12:28).

      (2) Because He is the same, therefore a Christian may
always count on Him for adequate supply of every
material and spiritual need, and the strength to
come triumphantly through every crisis (as did the
deceased leaders just alluded to, who trusted that
God would never abandon them — v. 5 — and
would always empower them to overcome the
opposition of the world — v. 6).

   b. **(:9)** Adherence to the basic Gospel: because Christ is
the same, therefore God's revealed truth never changes,
and what has once been revealed by God as true may
be confidently adhered to and be found sufficient.

      (1) The danger: (a) manifold and varied teachings,
which human teachers venture to add to Scripture.
As varied *(poikilai)*, they are inconsistent and con-
tradictory, and stand in contrast to the marvelous

harmony of Scripture. (b) Strange *(xenai)* teachings, i. e. from some other source than God, and clashing with what God has revealed.

(2) The specific nature of the teachings now being foisted upon the Hebrew Christians at Rome: the O. T. regulations about food and drink, as still having a binding force.

(3) The fallacy of these teachings: they suggested that a Christian put some of his trust upon the efficacy of works (external observances, and those too which have no ethical significance and do not of themselves help those who follow them) instead of upon the direct grace of God, which is necessarily the constant and only foundation for a holy and God-pleasing life.

4. **(13:10-11)** The privilege of being separated with Christ apart from the world.

a. **(:10)** The O. T. sacrifices which these persistent Judaizers seek to re-impose have already been fulfilled by Christ on Calvary, where He offered up an effectual atonement. The partaking of this atoning sacrifice by faith elevates the N. T. believer to a far higher position of personal privilege than that of the Levitical priests, who ate of the sacrificial flesh of the sin-offering and the peace-offering. (Or else this verse may simply be referring to the spiritual food and drink of the benefits of Christ's body and blood, as contrasted with the mere physical food and drink, concerning which the Judaizing teachers were so zealously legislating.)

b. **(:11)** Being excluded from the sacrificial worship and fellowship of the Jews is perfectly acceptable, since that very exclusion is itself a fulfilment of the O. T. type of the Atonement sacrifice.

(1) On the Day of Atonement the bullock of Aaron's sin-offering and the goat of the Congregation's sin-offering were conveyed, after their blood had been sprinkled on the Mercy-seat, to a place outside the camp and were there consumed entirely by fire (Lev. 16:27).

(2) So also Christ, like the bullock and the goat, was offered up outside the city walls on the hill of Golgotha, having been rejected by the nation of the Jews.

c. **(:13)** Consequently we too, if Christians, are identified with Christ in His state of rejection, and therefore we remain outside the pale of Jewry, bearing
in our own persons the reproach of Christ.

d. **(:14)** This is only reasonable, for if we are not of this
world, we must not expect to be accepted by the world
as its proper citizens. Our true homeland is heaven and
the Messianic Kingdom to come, and towards this we
are to direct all our earnest attention.

5. **(13:15-17)** Heavenly citizenship involves the duties of
(a) thanksgiving (b) benevolence (c) obedience to
spiritual leaders.

a. **(:15)** As those who partake of the altar of Golgotha,
we N. T. priest-believers have just one kind of sacrifice
to offer up to God: the thank-offering. (Note that
gratitude constitutes the basic motive for all of Christian ethics and program of life — in contrast to the
worldling's motive of self-justification or merit-earning
or pursuit of personal pleasure or advantage.)

(1) This thank-offering (Heb. *tōwdah*) is to be offered
up spiritually (not materially) by the praise and
confession which we express with our lips (thus
fulfilling what Hosea 14:2-3 enjoined upon the
repentant Israel of the future, who are to pray to
Jehovah: "Take away all our iniquity . . . and we
shall render up our lips as bullock-offerings." The
reading "fruit of the lips" rests upon the omission
of one last letter of the Hebrew word for "bullocks," *pārīm,* which would allow the remaining
three consonants to be construed as *perī*, "fruit.")

(2) **(13:15b)** Therefore a constant duty and privilege
of the believer-priest is to call upon the name of
Jehovah, both in prayer and thank-offering, thereby proclaiming it as a testimony to others (a com-
plex of ideas involved in the word "giving thanks,"
homologeō, which is usually translated "confess";
but in Biblical usage, to confess to God's name
involves not only uttering it, but also recognizing
and proclaiming and praising it before others).

b. **(:16)** Another phase of the Christian's life of thanksgiving: benevolence and generosity to others. Here the
general word for kindly service, *eupoiia* ("to do
good"), is followed by *koinōnia* ("to communicate"),

which among other things suggests sharing with a brother in material need (as, for example, the Corinthian church sent a relief fund to the needy Christians in Jerusalem through Paul; cf. II Cor. 9:13, where *koinōnia* is translated "distribution"). With this twofold offering of spoken witness and practical loving-kindness God is well pleased.

c. **(:17)** Obedience to the leaders of the Church, the apostles, pastors, elders and deacons, is also necessary for pleasing the Lord.

(1) As they have been previously exhorted (v. 7) to remember and follow the example of godly leaders now deceased, they are here admonished to obey and submit to those leaders who are now over them.

(2) This duty of obedience is a fair requirement since the church officers themselves bear a heavy responsibility before God, that they be faithful in feeding and guarding the sheep; for this stewardship they will have to give a solemn accounting before God.

(3) This is a duty which involves the denial of personal comfort and tranquility of mind; they are like the watchmen who guard the city walls at night.

(4) Note that church-officers are required in a very real sense to identify themselves with the interests and concerns of the congregation, providing to the flock a godly example of a Christ-centered life.

(5) They will be able to render their accounting to the Lord with joy if they see the members of the church growing in the knowledge of the Lord and bearing fruit in His service. But if they see them backward and carnally minded, they will be constrained to grieve over them and groan in intercessory prayer for them — an injurious and discreditable thing for the wayward ones who occasion them this concern.

6. **(13:18-25)** Concluding requests and benedictions.

a. **(:18-19)** Prayer request of the apostle himself (related to the solemn duty resting upon church-officers) : pray for me, that I may be prospered in the Lord's work and be enabled to return to Rome.

(1) The Hebrew Christians may legitimately intercede for him, for his conscience is clear of any unconfessed and unrepented sin ("good conscience"), and his sincere purpose is to live a Christ-honoring life before all observers.

(2) Specifically, they are to pray that hindrances may be removed from his return to Rome, where he hopes to take up anew his ministry of building up his readers in the faith.

b. **(:20-21)** His prayer for them: their being perfected in the performance of the will of God.

(1) "The God of Peace" — just what the Hebrew Christians needed in the critical times in which they lived, when pressures bore down upon them from within and from without, both to separate from their true spiritual leaders under the stress of unexpected afflictions, and to question the power of Christ Himself and the efficacy of His finished work.

(2) **(13:20b)** How God has brought about this peace: by what He did for His Son, raising Him up from the dead, thus (a) signalizing victory over death — the penalty for sin — and guaranteeing eternal life; (b) raising up all those who are united with Christ by faith.

(3) That Christ's resurrection was not for Himself only but for those also united with Him by faith, is suggested by His pastoral relation to Christians: "the great Shepherd of the sheep" (who once went astray, but who have been discovered and brought back).

(4) **(13:20c)** The basis for Christ's resurrection along with His sheep: the Covenant sealed with His life's blood; a Covenant eternal because it has fully satisfied all the requirements of God's love and holiness and justice, and there will by consequence be no added requirement necessary either to perfect it or to keep it perfect.

(5) **(13:21a)** The desired result of this resurrection-power: to make the believer himself perfect, or thoroughly equipped and altogether confirmed in his Christ-character (*katartizo* — "fit all the joints together: make complete") in all departments of

his life — no blind spots in his vision or areas of inconsistency in his conduct.

(6) **(13:21b)** The end result, the validating goal for all that has gone before: the accomplishment of God's own perfect will, which is only brought to pass through those of His servants who voluntarily yield themselves in love, to be used in whatever way He may choose.

   (a) God's *will* here contemplates especially those things which the indwelling Christ accomplishes through those who are wholly yielded to Him, for it is those things which are preeminently well-pleasing *(euareston)* to the Father (who stated at Christ's baptism, "This is My beloved Son, in whom I am *well pleased"*).

(7) **(13:21c)** The accomplishment of God's perfect will is always attended by the manifestation of God's glory — the highest and noblest aim that can possibly be prayed for by any Christian — that eternal glory which now irradiates heaven and which shines through to earthlings whenever an obedient human heart lives for God alone.

c. **(13:22)** Exhortation to receive the author's teaching with faith and love.

(1) Although this letter contains words of rebuke which may grieve the readers, they ought to bear up under them (take them in good part), in view of the love and prayerful interest he feels towards them, which has prompted him to write them this letter.

(2) "In a few words" — He could have written at far greater length and with much greater plainness upon their guilt of unbelief and peril of apostasy, than he actually has done. (He does not mean to imply that this letter as a whole is a brief one.)

d. **(13:23)** Personal item of news concerning Timothy. Timothy (of Paul's intimate circle of acquaintance, a circle which must include the author also, whether he be Apollos or Barnabas or some other) has recently been released from imprisonment, and they both plan to visit the readers (at Rome?) soon.

e. **(13:24)** Final greeting: 1) to the church-leaders (pastors, elders and deacons) ; 2) to the congregation in general. This greeting is conveyed to them from the residents of Italy (*hoi apo tēs Italias* — "those who are from Italy") who happen to be in the city where the author is sojourning, and where presumably Timothy has been imprisoned.

f. **(13:25)** Final prayer that God's grace may abide with them all (supplying all the spiritual needs indicated in the letter).